FIDELIS

THE
MARINES

THE MARINES

PHOTOGRAPHED BY ANTHONY EDGEWORTH
WRITTEN BY JOHN DE ST. JORRE

DOUBLEDAY
NEW YORK   LONDON   TORONTO   SYDNEY   AUCKLAND
1989

Excerpt from "My First Twenty-Four Hours as a Marine"
Reprinted by permission of International Creative Management, Inc.
Copyright © 1986 by William Broyles, Jr.

Published by Doubleday, a division of
Bantam Doubleday Dell Publishing Group, Inc.
666 Fifth Avenue, New York, New York 10103

Library of Congress Cataloging-in-Publication Data

De St. Jorre, John, 1936-
The marines.

1. United States. Marine Corps—Pictorial works
I. Edgeworth, Anthony.   II. Title.
VE23.D43   1989   359.9'6'0973   88-30934

ISBN 0-385-23683-2

Text copyright © 1989 by John de St. Jorre
Photographs copyright © 1989 by Anthony Edgeworth
All Rights Reserved
Design: Samuel N. Antupit

CONTENTS

Preceding pages
Sunset Parade: 8th and
I Marine Barracks ceremo-
nial unit at the Iwo Jima
Memorial
Young marines training
at the School of Infantry:
Camp Lejeune, North Carolina
An LVTP-7 amphibious
assault vehicle (AAV) — generically
known as an "amtrac,"
from "amphibious tractor" —
launches off Onslow Beach,
North Carolina
The Marine Corps' globe
and anchor emblem was designed
in 1868 and first worn
the following year. Its design
was influenced by the
British Royal Marines' insignia
of a globe and laurel. This
insignia is at the entrance of
the Marine Barracks in
Washington, D.C.
Cold weather warfare
AV-8B Harrier "jump jets"
on an improvised desert
airstrip at Surprise Springs:
29 Palms, California. The
Harrier fighter can land and
take off vertically or
become airborne using a
short runway
A CH-53 Sea Stallion, the
marines' largest helicopter,
returning to base
Senior drill instructors,
Marine Corps Recruit Depot:
San Diego, California
A marine general officer's
full-honors funeral: Arlington
National Cemetery
Front endpaper: **A**rchitectural
detail, Center Walk: 8th and I
Marine Barracks, Washington, D.C.
Back endpaper: **D**etail of CH-46
helicopter

The photographs in this book were
taken with Nikon cameras and Nik-
kor lenses in formats ranging from
20mm to 600mm. Mr. Edgeworth
used Kodak films exclusively in producing these photographs.

FOREWORD

The United States Marine Corps, older than the Republic itself by a year, is as familiar to the average American as the flag. The marines symbolize, more than any other part of the nation's armed forces, discipline, valor, patriotism, and military virtue. Their presence is felt beyond the barracks, the fleet, and the battlefield. In Washington, they perform a unique ceremonial role and are the President's musicians; around the world they guard United States embassies. The characteristics distinguishing them from the rest of the American military, provoking a medley of emotions that encompass reverence, envy, and disdain, are shared by all military elites since the time of Sparta. The marines are, as they say, looking for a few good men—and they mean it.

In democratic nations all military institutions of this kind tend to be regarded ambivalently by the society from which they spring. The marines have their critics and their problems. They are too bulletheaded and square for some; too narcissistic and gung ho for others. They may look smart, be good at drill, and play superb martial music, say others, but so what? There are thousands of women marines, but the corps does not seem to have come to terms with them in its ranks or how the female component should be reconciled with its manly image. (They don't often say they are looking for a few good *women*.) Some people question the Marine Corps' military value, even its existence as a separate entity in the armed forces, a status that the corps has successfully sustained since Samuel Nicholas, the first marine officer, took up his commission during the Revolutionary War. Surely, the critics argue, the marines are obsolete, at best a colorful anachronism, at worst a military dinosaur. Iwo Jima was great stuff in its day, but who storms heavily defended beaches in the era of Star Wars?

Yet few Americans would willingly consign the marines to oblivion, for the United States Marine Corps has, through its long life and its own bootstrap efforts, entered into the national psyche of a country that tends to revere but not preserve its history. The phenomenon is reflected in the language: "Tell that to the marines!" "Send in the marines." "Once a marine, always a marine."

With a strength of almost two hundred thousand men and women, the Marine Corps is neither too small to be overlooked—or, worse still, absorbed by the other services—nor too big to lose its special identity and flavor. A separate service under the Department of the Navy and answerable to its civilian head, the Marine Corps still enjoys a considerable degree of autonomy. The only component of the armed forces whose existence and minimum size are prescribed by law, the corps has its own budget, its own headquarters, bases, training facilities, equipment, and so on. Its military boss and godfather is a four-star marine general who, as commandant of the United States Marine Corps, is a member of the Joint Chiefs of Staff, sharing equal status with the army, navy, and the air force.

The Marine Corps is structured and equipped for projecting American military power onto hostile shores from the sea and for rapid deployment to hot spots around the world. Its uniqueness, in the United States and indeed throughout the world, lies in its integrated nature as a fighting force. Larger than most nations' armies, the marines have their own infantry, artillery, tanks, aviation (fighters, reconnaissance, helicopters, and transports), and supplies. With logistical backup from the navy and air force, the Marine Corps has a formidable reach and a devastating punch.

A quintessentially American institution, the Marine Corps embodies the idealism, innocence, and manly virtue of the early Republic. The corps is still the ultimate proving ground for American youth, the place where little guys often surprise big guys, where sons catch up to their fathers, where a nobody becomes a somebody. The

Officer's campaign cover. This quintessential piece of marine headgear is only worn by drill instructors at the Parris Island and San Diego recruit depots and by members of Marine Corps shooting teams. Enlisted men wear a black patent leather band around the crown; officers are distinguished by gold braid and tassels

Marine Corps is not elitist: you do not have to know someone, or be the son of someone, to get in. And once in, you can make it all the way to the top, as the current commandant did. For many it is the first and most important rite of passage of manhood. For others it is the ultimate personal challenge, a total experience. "If you're Marine," wrote Lieutenant General Lewis "Chesty" Puller, one of the corps' greatest heroes, "you're all Marine."

The marine presence is pervasive in the broader society, in business, industry, the professions, even in politics. Marines, unlike people who have served in the other branches of the military, tend to retain their "marineness" when they leave the service. Conscious of having belonged to something special, they look out for each other when they go out into the civilian world.

Despite a rapidly changing world, the marines retain their Norman Rockwell flavor. Even their appearance sustains the dated image: flinty, crew-cutted, square-jawed tough guys who hit the beach first and hold it. But while the marines hark back to the Republic's origins with their naval phraseology, their high-necked uniforms, and their stirring music, they also see themselves on the cutting edge of modern warfare. Above all, they believe in professionalism, and the payoff is status. All marines believe that they are good, damn good, the best.

This is a book by outsiders, a writer, photographer, and designer who were only marginally military men and never served in the Marine Corps. It is essentially a work of reportage on the contemporary corps, a candid look at who the U.S. Marines are, what they do, and how they do it. Implicit in the story, however, is a question: are the marines as good as they say they are?

General Paul X. Kelley, who was commandant when we began the project and who granted us access to the corps, wrote to us saying: "As Marines, we don't purport to be perfect, but we put forth as pure an effort as I believe is humanly possible in order that we might live up to the expectations we know people have of us." His successor, General Alfred M. Gray, Jr., endorsed our access and General Kelley's sentiments. We have looked closely at the purity of the effort and the results. What we have seen and heard are between these pages.

While guiding the story, we have largely left judgments to the marines themselves. There is a lively debate within the corps that embraces most controversial topics, although the ranks of the principal debaters tend to tail off at the level of major or lieutenant colonel. After that, officers often have their eyes on their star and are reluctant to stick their necks out. The debate inside and outside the corps during the period of our research was intensified by several traumatic events, notably the Beirut bombing disaster and its post-mortem; the roles of Oliver North and Robert McFarlane, both former marines, in the Iran-Contra scandal; and the Moscow embassy marine security guard affair. All of these hurt the corps and individual marines, not least because the corps is a tight institution and because it places itself on a pedestal from which the occasional fall is all the more painful.

It is perhaps worth saying what this book is not. It is not a debate about whether there should be a marine corps or, indeed, a military in the United States. It is not an "official" or "authorized" account. We were given access to marine units without any commitments of any kind from either side. Our purpose was not to produce a military manual, a historical record, or a scholarly assessment of the Marine Corps. Those themes have been covered well and often. Yet elements of a manual, history, and a balance sheet are present because they are inescapable and important in any attempt to record the reality of the modern Marine Corps. What we think is different is our collective approach that derives from writer, photographer, and designer traveling and working closely together. The aim is to capture the special flavor of the United States Marine Corps in images and words. We adopted the same approach, with the same goal, for *The Guards,* our book on another famous military organization, and plan to do so in a project on the French Foreign Legion. With *The Guards,* it seemed to work. Whether it does here is for the reader to decide.

ACKNOWLEDGEMENTS

Our first debt is to the countless marines who went out of their way to help us. It would be impossible to thank them individually, and we have, in any case, adopted a policy of anonymity throughout much of the book. Almost without exception we found marines, whatever their rank, to be accessible, candid, and friendly. We thank them for their time, enthusiasm, and knowledge.

The project would not have been possible without the cooperation of the Marine Corps itself. General P. X. Kelley, commandant when it was launched, gave us the access we needed and his encouragement to do our job as thoroughly as possible. General Alfred M. Gray, Jr., his successor, whom we had met earlier in Norway, endorsed General Kelley's decision. Neither endorsement implied agreement with or responsibility for the final product. The buck stops with us, not with Marine Corps headquarters. We would like to express our deep appreciation to Generals Kelley and Gray for their personal interest and support.

The marines are famous—some would say, notorious—for their sense of publicity. But, as with all public affairs, it is a tough job when the aim is to reconcile two conflicting desires: to produce a good story yet at the same time cover one's rear end. We were lucky in coinciding with two superb and sensitive officers who successively held the difficult post of director of public affairs of the United States Marine Corps. Major General D.E.P. Miller got us started, and Brigadier General Walter Boomer bore the brunt, seeing us through to the end and performing many unsung acts above and beyond the call of duty. We thank them and their staffs around the globe for a job well done.

A number of individuals, active duty and former marines, helped us more than they probably realized and enlivened our working days. Our thanks are due to George Hunt, William Ketcham, Major General Raymond Murray, Colonel Martin Brandtner, James Webb, Master Sergeant Richard Pittman, Colonel Donald Myers, Colonel David Willis, Lieutenant Colonel Wheeler Baker, Captain Kelly McCann, Master Gunnery Sergeant Richard Carlisle, Brigadier General Matthew Caulfield, Lieutenant Colonel Arn Manella, Major Bob Watts, and Colonel John Greenwood, most of whom appear in the book in one shape or form. We owe a special debt of gratitude to Colonel John Ripley for his insights, his help in getting us where we needed to go, and his good company; to Colonel John Miller for his critical eye and wise advice; to Lieutenant Colonel Kevin Kennedy for his sharp and humorous observations and his ability to convey the special joy of being a marine; and to Lieutenant Colonel Doug Black for his balance and sense of humanity.

There is no magic formula for transforming the raw material of a book such as this into the finished artifact, just a lot of hard work. We would like to thank Joan Fisher, the copy editor, for her painstaking attention and helpful criticism of the text and Lisa Govan of The Sarabande Press for her limitless patience with the layout.

The list would not be complete without a tribute to Jody Harcourt, Tony Edgeworth's studio manager. Wherever we went—into the snows of Norway, the dust of the Mojave Desert, the jungles of the Philippines—Jody went too, lugging cameras and organizing our lives. She also brought more than a modicum of wisdom, wit, and charm to the enterprise, as well as an armor-plated sense of humor. We are very grateful.

John de St. Jorre and Anthony Edgeworth
New York City, August 1988

A.M. Bolognese & Sons, tailor and haberdasher to the marines since 1918: Potomac Avenue, Quantico

An unwarlike Marine
is quite as
unthinkable as an
honest burglar.

H.L. MENCKEN

PART 1:
THE MAKING OF A MARINE

Overleaf
The "motivation platoon": Marine Corps Recruit Depot, Parris Island, South Carolina, 1974. This method of producing the right attitude from recalcitrant or backsliding recruits is no longer in use

Recruiting: Times Square, New York City

It is a bitterly cold January day outside the tacky U.S. Armed Forces recruiting station in Times Square. The building, a shack on an island whose shores are washed by a never-ending flow of traffic and human flotsam, has been used to recruit young men and women into the armed forces since the early part of World War II.

The city owns the building, but it is maintained by the army's Corps of Engineers. Recruiting men to go to war, the office itself is no stranger to combat: a fire bomb was hurled through a window by antiwar protesters in the early 1970's, and the place almost burned down. Above it, amid the urgent neon messages of Times Square, the Stars and Stripes, sagging on a rusting pole, looks as defeated as some of the faces of the people who pass beneath it.

"People will stop you and say it's a disgrace," said a Marine Corps recruiting sergeant. "And they're right."

Disgrace or not, the four services (army, navy, air force, and the marines) do their thing inside. Each service has a corner and a desk and a slogan that tells you something about the differences between them. "Be All You Can Be," says the army; "It's Not Just A Job, It's An Adventure," proclaims the navy; "Aim High," exhorts the air force. Only the marines seem to reject the implication of career enhancement with the deadpan message: "We're Looking For A Few Good Men."

The marines' appeal to pride and tradition is underscored by the NCO's immaculate uniforms and their bearing. Not that they recruit any more than the other services—three to four new recruits each a month seems to be the average for all four branches. But the Marine Corps' message is clear to a young man and a young woman who have recently signed up and are in the office to explain why they did such a crazy thing.

"Most of my family went into the army," says the young man who is wearing a button that alleges "The More I Drink, the Better I Look." "I've always had it easy at home and school, but now I want something tougher. I kind of idolize Parris Island [marine boot camp]. It turned out a lot of good guys. I have a friend who has just finished there and it changed him completely."

This young fellow, who lives in Harlem, is already partly a marine, having joined a high school cadet program. He says that some of the kids on the block call him a weekend warrior and occasionally throw bottles at the cadets. His father wanted him to go to college first but he intends to do it the other way around.

The young woman, from Harlem, too, is also attracted by the training and the discipline. Neatly dressed and carrying a Louis Vuitton bag, she says she is working out to prepare herself physically for Parris Island, although that, in her opinion, is not the most important thing.

"You've got to have the right mind set," she says. "I want the challenge and I think I can do it. My friends tell me I'll never make it. The guys laugh most but they also say, 'Hell no, not for me.'"

She expects some male hassle in the marines, too. "You can't avoid it," she says, "but you just have to beat them at their own game—be better than they are."

She decided to go into the services in the tenth grade and on the marines a year later. But why the marines?

"I didn't want things to come too easily," she replies. "The marines have the best discipline, and people show them the most respect. They also have the best uniform," she adds as an afterthought.

Life in the shack on the square isn't too stressful most of the time. Nine out of ten of the people who come in are looking for directions, buying theater tickets, or, more urgently, in need of a bathroom. "It's Wendy's or Nathan's on opposite sides of Broadway," says a marine sergeant. "Take your pick."

But recruiting is big business in the Marine Corps, consuming large sums of money, manpower, and, in many cases, recruiters' nervous systems. A former commandant likened recruiting to combat in that there is constant stress and pressure.

"When there's not a real war on," says a captain who spent three years at the job, "it's the only war in town."

Recruiters are expected to make their quotas, although some officers fight shy of the term.

"What counts in the end, whatever you call it," says an officer who did three years of recruiting duty, "is throwing the feet on those yellow footprints painted on the road where the recruits are first received at boot camp."

There is a feedback system from the Marine Corps' two recruit training depots (one in Parris Island, South Carolina; the other in San Diego, California) to ensure that recruiters do not sweep unsuitable people into their nets by selling them the wrong image of the corps. An unusually high attrition rate at boot camp can be just as bad for a recruiter as failure to meet his quota.

To join the marines you have to be a high school graduate (or the equivalent), have a clean police record, be between 4' 10" and 6' 7", and pass the physical examination and some simple written tests.

While the recruiters are explaining this, a man in his mid-forties comes in to ask for a marines car sticker. He is a former marine, a Vietnam veteran who now runs a health club on Fifty-seventh Street. He thanks the sergeant for the sticker and says it might help deter car thieves who have also been in the corps.

Difficulties arise not only in trying to make quotas but in marines being detached from their natural habitat in an isolated, potentially dangerous civilian environment, where wine, women, and song are the order of the day.

"The real problem," says an officer, "is not being a marine out there."

What's recruiting like?

For an officer, it's a job of immense responsibility commanding large resources, including a budget that may run into hundreds of thousands of dollars. One former recruiter compared the job with that of a district sales manager for a big corporation, the differences being that the marine manager is usually much younger than his commercial counterpart and his "sales" are calculated in human bodies rather than in dollars and cents.

"Potential recruits are usually deathly afraid of boot camp." he says. "In any case, it's hard to convince a kid to give up his life for three years and maybe altogether. That's a tough sell. It's a bittersweet duty: bitter with the day-to-day pressures and frustrations, but sweet when you find some good people for the corps."

"The first thing you've got to know is how serious a person is about joining, otherwise you waste a hell of a lot of time," says a recruiting sergeant who has been at it for a couple of years. "You have to get to know them really well, go to their homes, and all that kind of stuff. It's a hard job."

Does he enjoy it?

"It's certainly unique," he says and then pauses. "At times, too unique."

Overleaf
Where it all begins

Boot Camp: Parris Island, South Carolina

It's 2:00 A.M. on Parris Island, South Carolina. The Greyhound bus, its interior lights off, sits motionless at the curbside. At first it is not clear whether there is anyone inside. Then, in the lights of the receiving barracks, a shadowy profile with a low-crowned hat tilted at a threatening angle can be seen moving down the aisle.

U.S. MARINE CORP
PARRIS ISLAND

A puff of wind, carrying the smell of saltwater marshes and decay, rustles the pines. Silence.

"GET OFF THE FREAKIN' BUS. MOVE!"

The explosive violence of the next few minutes can be compared to the first shock of combat, the awesome moment when one phalanx of cavalry crashes into another, when an artillery barrage finds its target, when an ambush is sprung. At least so it probably seems to the thirty-five young men who spring off that bus and line up in the road on the sets of yellow footprints, painted in columns of threes, each pair at the approved 45 degree angle. Thus begins the boiling down of a human being who has been brave or dumb enough to submit voluntarily to the heat. The resulting liquid—a curious mixture of fear, wonderment, pain, and pride—is poured into a new and distinctive mold labeled "marine."

The man underneath the low-crowned olive-green hat has been joined by two more drill instructors who snap and snarl like ill-fed huskies around the young men on the street. The senior DI, a diminutive, tight-waisted black sergeant with the voice of an enraged bull, marches the recruits up into the new red brick receiving barracks. An officer, watching the scene, leans over and whispers: "Mighty Mouse."

"Now you're walking faster than humanly possible," the DI roars. "Move it!"

The doors open and the recruits pass under a chrome crossbar that tells them: "Through these Portals Pass Prospects for America's Finest Fighting Force. United States Marines." Their indoctrination has begun.

The recruits sit at school desks, heads down, hands on the backs of their heads, as the documentation process gets under way. The three DI's hand out forms and—through a mixture of threat, kindergarten step-by-step advice, and occasional help—guide the platoon through its first tactical, albeit bureaucratic, maneuver.

"Take this form and get away from me. Take out the magic marker and throw the paper on the freakin' deck and write your platoon number, 1054, on the back of your nonwriting hand. Put the daggone mailing address there. If you don't have a telephone number, I want you to write the word 'none,' N-O-N-E. Put your finger on the next box. Not above. Not below. Not to the right. Not to the left. Do it NOW!"

There is a growing pile of paper on the floor under the recruits' feet. The group is a representative cross section of American boys. They come from all over the country; there are blacks, Hispanics, Asians, Catholics, Protestants, and Jews. They are dressed in the uniform of modern youth: jeans, leather jackets, loose colorful shirts, sneakers. Several have long hair, one with glossy locks tumbling onto his shoulders.

They look well fed—too well fed in some cases. No one comes into the corps these days because he is in need of a square meal or a pair of shoes. They are healthy, normal-looking kids—Norman Rockwell would be reassured were he around. Marine Corps statistics say that the average recruit is eighteen years old, 5′ 9″ in height, weighs 158 pounds, and is a high school graduate, a physically smaller and intellectually larger specimen than the conventional image of the marine grunt.

Most of them seem well prepared for their ordeal and are awed but not scared. A few, however, are already in trouble, not following the orders, mislaying items, looking desperately lost. One boy is visibly trembling; another, a big blond kid who the DI's believe is a foreigner due to his accent, is showing signs of aggression. (He later turns out to be a New Yorker.)

A recruit nervously scratches himself. Mighty Mouse pounces. "No one said scratch, NO ONE SAID SCRATCH!" he screams.

Roughly 15 percent of the thirty-five aspiring marines in the room won't make it. But is there also a future commandant of the United States Marine Corps here? The man who became the twenty-ninth commandant was once a "boot" at Parris Island.

A DI stands menacingly over a befuddled recruit.

"Write 'mother,'" he bellows.

"OK"

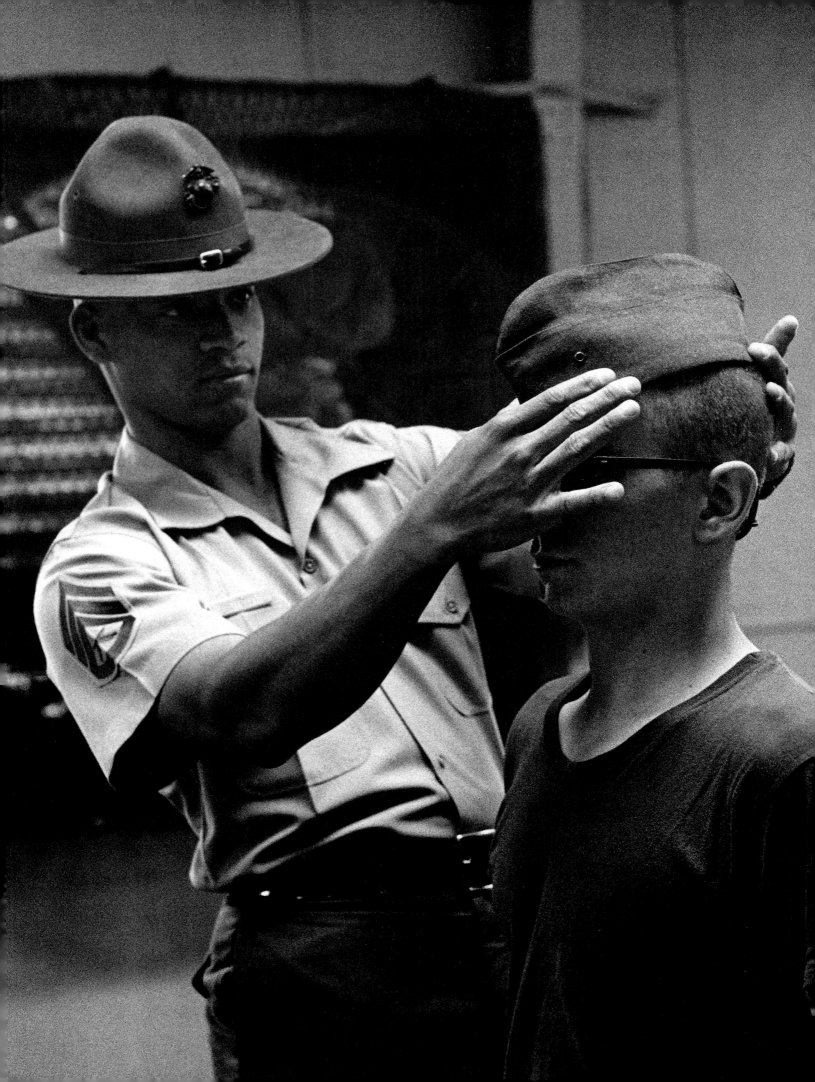

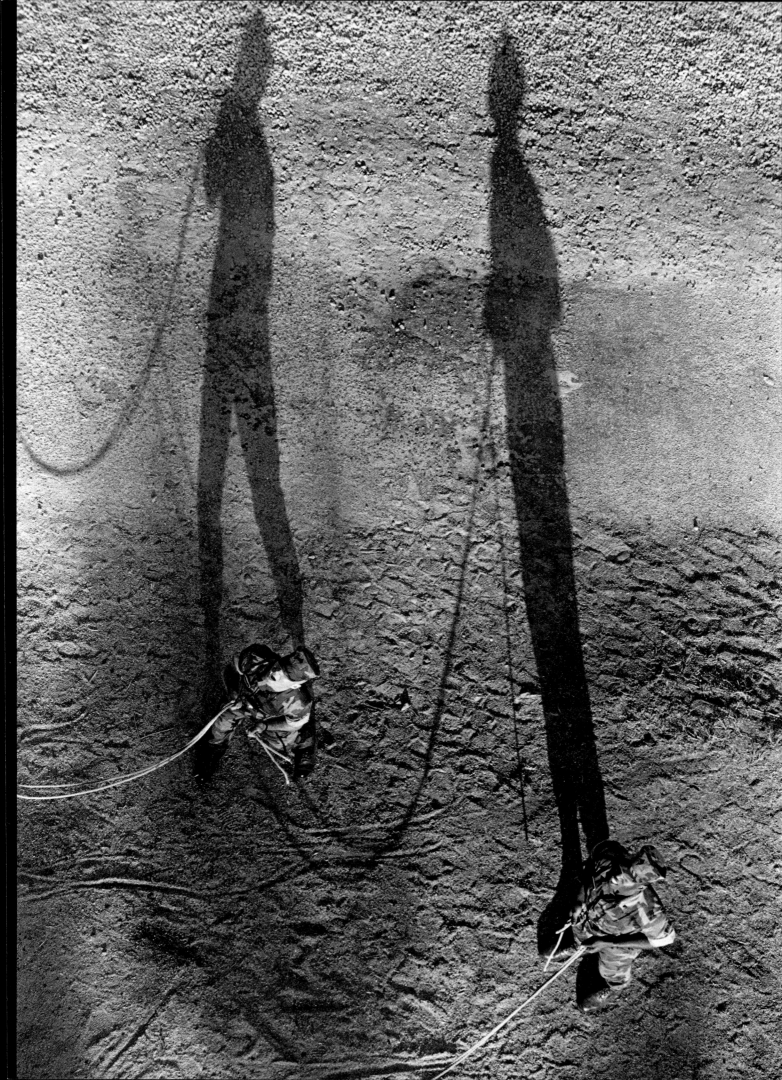

"OK my butt. YES, SIR."

"Yes, sir!"

There is a frantic tearing sound as the recruits, on the order, rip open plastic bags and decant two combination padlocks on their desks with a clatter.

Mighty Mouse paces up and down, giving instructions.

"Hold the number up in front of your face and memorize it. MEMORIZE IT. Get it into your freakin' brain structure, and don't come to us saying you don't know it, jeopardizing our time." He brings the flat of his hand down on a recruit's desk with a crash. "Memorize it!"

One recruit can't open his padlock. Like the rest he is afraid to expose himself, fearful of standing out. Anonymity, as most of the young men in the room have already learned, is the key to boot camp and to survival. One of the other DIs spots the trouble and solves the problem. "Don't thank me," he growls when the flushed recruit mumbles his gratitude.

The divestment of personality and possessions continues. The recruits line up and hand over the contents of their pockets. The DIs look more scornful than ever as they check through the harvest and toss most of it into large garbage cans in front of them. One of the DIs holds up a condom in the face of a recruit. "What's this contraband? What are you going to use this for down here?" Another recruit surrenders hair-growing pills. One kid has $140 on him. All money and valuables are taken away and returned to the recruits when they leave the island. Another boy parts with a five-dollar bill, which you sense his mother had pressed into his hand just before he left.

The first phase is over. The recruits line up in the street outside for their first real march, albeit to breakfast. The time is 4:30 A.M. Inside, Mighty Mouse relaxes and takes off his distinctive Smokey the Bear hat ("campaign cover" in Marinese). Suddenly, he is a different man. He is not much more than a kid himself, a twenty-four year old with an engaging smile. "Been easy on them to get them through the process," he says in a surprisingly soft voice. "Low stress."

A group of two-day-old recruits, their skulls an unpleasant whitish gray from the recent shearing, finish cleaning up. Mighty Mouse puts his cover back on, deftly adjusting the brown strap at the back and tilting the brim forward. His arm shoots out, index finger as rigid as a pistol barrel.

"Get away from me. Five, four, three, two, one. GET OUT OF MY FACE."

Mr. Hyde is back. Dr. Jekyll is nowhere to be seen.

In the mess hall, the recruits eat their first marine meal, or "chow," as they will call it for the rest of their marine life.

"Put your banana on the tray and hold it with two hands. No one is going to take your banana away. DON'T LOOK AT ME."

The DIs scurry around, snapping, barking, nagging. "Keep the line tight, keep the line tight." Even something a recruit has learned from infancy, such as conveying food from plate to mouth, is monitored and given a new military meaning. "Put your feet flat on the deck at 45 degrees and eat with one hand. You're an American, not a barbarian." The food is plentiful and varied; the problem at this stage is the appetite. When they have finished, the recruits sit at attention facing each other in silence.

Back at the receiving barracks, they receive their gear. A female civilian, who is every bit as intimidating as the DIs (it turns out she is married to a master sergeant), paces up and down on a raised walkway, supervising the issue.

"Who doesn't have an ink pen? Raise your hand."

Recruits write down their platoon and Social Security numbers for the umpteenth time. The good lady marches up and down the line of sea bags, clothing, and PX articles. Things are not going quickly or smoothly enough for her taste. Some recruits are confused and talking to each other. "Shut the fuck up," one hisses to another who is getting on his case. Exasperation mounts. The lady speaks as if to congenital idiots: "Get your [pause] bag [pause] on the floor!"

The PX issue includes soap, razor blades, toothpaste, shoe brushes, writing materials, *Leatherneck* magazine, and insect repellent (for Parris Island's notorious "no-see-ums," sand fleas that bite like the devil), as well as some rather surprising items such as cotton swabs (for cleaning the M-16 rifle), mouthwash, and deodorant. Shampoo is conspicuous by its absence.

Three civilian barbers in short yellow jackets stand ready, shears in hand, in the barber's shop. Two garbage cans are placed beside the barbers' chairs, which face away from the mirrors so the victims cannot see what is happening. The recruits line up, and this most symbolic rite of passage begins. The shearing is done in great sweeps from the base of the skull to the forehead. Most barbers can despatch a recruit in thirty seconds or less.

A shorn recruit stands over each garbage can and wipes the head of the newly cut with a towel moistened with water from a nearby bottle. One of these acolytes has difficulty removing surplus hair from a gleaming skull and reaches for the water bottle. A DI bears down on him.

"You blessing him or something? Use the daggone towel!"

He whips around to someone else who shows reluctance. "Get over here and get your head scraped. DON'T LOOK AT ME!"

It is now 5 A.M. The long night continues with showering (by number: "soap and rinse your crotch," etc.), a lecture on hygiene, an issue of bedding with instruction on how to make the bed in the approved marine fashion, the removal of civilian clothes for the duration of their stay, the replacing of eyeglasses with the Marine Corps' standard issue (dark-framed glasses with straight wings), and so on throughout the new day until, fifteen hours after the Greyhound bus brought them to the yellow footprints, they collapse onto their "racks" and sleep the sleep of the dead.

Modern Parris Island is full of surprises. Old-timers would find new red brick structures rapidly replacing the Second World War two-story white wooden buildings. There are many more officers around than they remembered. They would find strange, strict regulations against foul language and manhandling recruits. They would think it curious to see vans with stretchers and medical corpsmen following every run and route march, or recruits massaging their armpits with deodorant sticks before donning their utilities, or even women marines jumping off the forty-five-foot rappelling tower. (Women marines, for God's sake!)

The general public would be equally surprised. Weaned on the old image, the public's beliefs were reinforced perhaps by the long boot camp sequence in Stanley Kubrick's film *Full Metal Jacket,* in which the DI is played by a former real life DI whose inventive four-letter-laden patter is matched by the bursts of physical violence he inflicts on his recruits.

"People say Parris Island has changed," says a senior officer. "The world has changed." In the old days—the days of the "old corps"—the world used to change, too, albeit slowly, but Parris Island slower still. Established in 1915 as a regular recruit-training depot, Parris Island has its own institutional memory and its own way of doing things. But, not surprisingly, its history reflects the changing nature of the broader society.

Between the two world wars, for instance, the young men joining the Marine Corps tended to be physically hardened, self-reliant farm boys. The flavor of Parris Island in those days is captured by the story of the DI who greeted his new recruits with a challenge: he would take anyone on and lick him. To his dismay, half the platoon stepped forward, and he beat a tactical retreat.

During World War II, a huge influx of men strained the resources of the system but produced relatively little brutality and abuse. It was only after the Korean War that serious problems began to develop. With very little officer supervision, poorly paid and overworked DIs, eager to get results, took the law into their own hands. Hazing, maltreatment, corruption, and random brutality became commonplace. Physical abuse included punching recruits in the stomach, burning them with cigarettes, stacking wayward recruits into trash bins, and making them run a gauntlet of belt-swinging fellow recruits.

Much of this came to light in 1956 when a drill instructor, who was apparently under stress from a painful back injury but who also had been drinking, took his platoon on a punitive night march through Ribbon Creek, the tidal marshland behind the rifle range on Parris Island. Six recruits drowned and all hell broke loose.

The subsequent congressional hearings, Marine Corps investigation, court martial, and huge media coverage led to an intensive self-examination. But the corps was allowed to clean up its own act. While the basic elements of training were not changed, many of the more abusive methods were banned, more officers were brought in to supervise the DIs, and the latters' conditions of service were improved. (The Smokey the Bear campaign hat was reintroduced to improve morale.)

But the 1960s and early 1970s were difficult years for Marine Corps recruit training. The advent of the "permissive society," the Vietnam War and its sour aftermath, racial tension and turmoil, and difficult transitions from an all-volunteer force to the draft and back again strained the system. Most of the DIs still believed that high stress and rough and tough tactics did the job best.

A measure of this is well caught in Herb Moore's meticulous account of his boot camp experiences at Parris Island in the early 1960s in his book *Rows of Corn.* He describes his senior drill instructor's method of dealing with "disciplinary problems." There were two options, the DI told the recruits. First, "by the book," which meant that disciplinary breaches would be reported in the approved manner under the Uniform Code of Military Justice, and, more likely than not, each misdemeanor would end up on the recruit's permanent record.

The second way to handle these problems was "right here, in the platoon." The DIs would decide what punishment was justified and administer it themselves, "whether it's doing fifty push-ups, a fist in the stomach, or whatever." The DIs then withdrew, leaving seventy stunned young men to discuss the choice that had been thrust upon them and to vote on it. On returning the senior DI made it clear that this was the recruits' one and only chance to have a say in the matter, and that the vote would have to be unanimous. By a show of hands the platoon put themselves at the mercy of their instructors.

Still displaying a sense of shock when he wrote this account two decades later, Moore comments: "We had voted, freely and democratically, to give dictatorial powers to three men none of us knew. If only we could have known — really known — what was to follow, I'm sure there would have been votes by some of the recruits to go by the book."

The result of these methods was further tragedy. In early 1976 a recruit, Lynn McClure, died from injuries sustained in a pugil stick bout at San Diego boot camp three months earlier. Three other recruits died about the same time from heat and other causes during training, and a fourth was shot in the hand by his drill instructor.

Once again there was a public furor but with a much more concerned Congress than during the Ribbon Creek affair, resulting in nine days of public hearings instead of one. Congress reviewed recruit training in all the services, which revealed more than twice as many incidents of abuse in the Marine Corps as in the army, navy, and air force combined. There was a probing, critical media and a skeptical public.

Once again there were courts martial, changes of command, reforms, internal controversy, and a deep soul searching. The McClure incident was even more serious than Ribbon Creek for the Marine Corps. Congress made it clear that the American public would not tolerate abuse of its young men and that if there were any more incidents of this kind, marine recruit training would be handed over to the army. To marines, from the commandant down to the DIs on the drill field, this would mean the end of the Marine Corps.

In the last decade, there has been a sea change in recruit training. A stroll around the depot would make that clear to old-timer and newcomer alike. The DIs do not curse, at least not on the drill field or in front of the recruits. Ironically, there is more bad language from the recruits themselves. Racial slurs and ethnic epithets are gone. (Some marines differentiate between their white and black comrades as "light green" and "dark green" marines, apparently without offense to either.)

A DI is not allowed to touch a recruit except to adjust his uniform, and only after having made his intention clear. Some DIs have been busted and taken off the drill field for even minor infractions of this rule, such as moving a recruit's head to the correct position by grasping his chin.

Officers seem to be everywhere, supervising and monitoring but occasionally becoming involved in some of the day-to-day work of training the recruits, a task that used to be left exclusively to the DIs.

While the basic relationship between recruit and DI appears to have remained unchanged, many important symbolic aspects of it have altered. The recruit no longer has to make a final clean breast of his past with the "moment of truth," when he traditionally had a last chance to clear up his record. The demarcation line between his civilian and military life is thus a little more gray than it used to be.

Senior DI's now have to stand in front of their new squads, under the eyes of their officers, and pledge that they will treat their charges with "firmness, fairness, dignity, and compassion." This is the Drill Instructor's Covenant, in which the DI promises not to threaten the recruit with physical harm, abuse, or harassment. He also tells the recruits to report acts of abuse or mistreatment to him, and if they believe he has mistreated them they are to report to the officer commanding the series.

The "motivation platoon," in which wayward recruits were punished in the most grueling, dramatic, and debasing manner without actually harming them, has gone. Punishment is now confined to strictly controlled and limited bursts of physical exercise (push-ups, etc.) known as "incentive physical training," or IPT. For the physically backward there is a remedial billet in the physical conditioning platoon.

For the unmotivated there is a slew of officers and the depot's resident psychiatrist to talk to. Remedy, if not total redemption, seems to be the idea behind all this, in order to save as many souls as possible even though some may be of dubious worth. The point is to keep the attrition rate as low as possible.

Training is shorter than it used to be but is still longer than army or air force boot camp. Much greater care is taken during South Carolina's stifling summer weather: recruits may be off the parade ground for days, even weeks, at a time due to the heat. There are diets for overweight recruits, air conditioning and television in the squad bays, and, in theory at least, eight hours of uninterrupted sleep at night, except for those on fire watch.

One of the most striking aspects of Parris Island today is its openness. Entering the depot one could be forgiven for thinking the place is a state park, complete with picnic benches under shady fir trees festooned with Spanish moss, overlooking the water. Congress, the media, the public, and the marines themselves have changed Parris Island from a remote and private marine backwater, where great and sometimes terrible things happened, into a fishbowl. Visitors pour in at the rate of two thousand a week.

Over on what is now euphemistically called the "confidence course," which bears a remarkable resemblance to a military assault or obstacle course, marine recruits are tackling the "slide for life." The task is to reach the ground safely from a thirty-foot-high platform connected to the ground by three ropes slung at an angle of about 45 degrees. To make it more interesting the recruits have to change their crawling or sliding position from on top of the rope to underneath it a couple of times on the way down. If they fall off at any stage there is a pool of cold muddy water waiting for them below.

A recruit, about twenty feet up, does just that as he loses control of the rope with his legs, hangs by his arms for an agonizing minute while vainly trying to kick his legs back up onto the rope, and hits the water with a mighty splash. The DIs yell at him unmercifully. Punishment is the ignominy of a very public failure and having to put his hands on his head and sing the Marine Corps hymn as he wades out of the pool.

"The point of it," says an officer, "is to develop upper body strength and confidence. It's also a macho thing; that's what they've read about before they joined the Marine Corps."

Down at the rifle range, recruits are learning the fundamentals of what many marines believe is their own special art form: marksmanship. Recruits learn to fire from sitting, kneeling, prone, and standing positions at targets two hundred, three hundred, and five hundred yards away. They spend two of their ten weeks at boot camp on the range. Range instructors, wearing pith helmets that recall marine uniforms of an earlier epoch, move up and down the line checking the recruits who are firing live ammunition for the first time.

"All ready on the firing line," comes a singsong voice from the control tower. There is a crackle of rifle fire, followed by a dry echo from the surrounding woods. The smell of cordite drifts over the line of prone recruits. "Cease fire, cease fire, unload and lock."

The instructors say that fear of the weapon and safety are the main problems although, eventually, most recruits are more scared of failing to qualify than anything else. The NCO's talk nostalgically among themselves about the old M-14 rifle. None liked its successor, the M-16A1; it was too light. Now they have the M-16A2, which has a heavier barrel and some other improvements. "But I loved the M-14," says a gunnery sergeant who used it in Vietnam. "You could bury it in mud and still shoot all day."

It's in the woods, and you don't really see it until you turn a corner. There it is. Merely looking at it turns your stomach over. It is Parris Island's rappelling tower, forty-five feet high, painted in Marine Corps scarlet and gold, with six ropes dangling loosely from its summit. Up there a squat, heavily tattooed drill instructor harangues a crowd of awestruck recruits who, in a few minutes, will have to jump off the tower, entrusting their lives during that swift and vertical descent to a canvas harness, a metal ring, and a piece of rope.

"There's two ways you can go down the wall," the DI bellows, "with your lips or your feet. We don't kiss the wall, understand?"

"Yes, SIR!" the recruits roar back from down below.

The drill instructor who has just demonstrated the Austrian rappel, diving off headfirst instead of the relatively sedate foot-first jump, looks around him. "There's nothing to it. New York trash moonwalk down buildings all the time."

The Holberton Tower, named after a staff sergeant who taught rappelling here and who was killed in Beirut, has two functions. There is the wall simulating a tall building from which a marine might have to get out in a hurry one day, and there is the free slide, representing a swift exit from a helicopter. Recruits have to do both rappels in order to graduate.

On top of the tower the recruits are lining up. There are four ropes down the wall and two dangling free for the straight drops. The technique is to slow the slide by pulling the rope into the small of the back with one hand while using the other to guide the descent. The "helicopter" rappel is the most fearful: first is the step forward into the void and then the drop before braking with the hand behind the back. But the wall, which requires a backward launch, demands more technique: during the descent the recruit must bounce off it with his feet and not his teeth.

One by one the recruits disappear over the side of the tower, shouting their names and chanting "off rappel" as they go. One recruit slides jerkily down the rope audibly muttering "Holy Mary, Mother of God" over and over again. The tattooed drill instructor peers closely at another recruit who momentarily hesitates. "You scared to death or something, recruit?" he yells. "GET OFF MY TOWER!"

Down below, each rope is belayed by a DI so that if a recruit panics and forgets to pull the rope into his back to slow his slide, the DI can move quickly backward pulling the rope, producing the same result.

All goes well until a solidly built recruit, wearing a pair of the grim PI-issue eyeglasses, refuses to jump. The DIs gather around him showering him with advice, exhortation, and, eventually, threats. "Take a step—close your eyes—be a man—look at the trees—go, recruit, go—trust us—shout 'Marine Corps' as loud as you can—one, two, three, go!—all your friends are waiting to get out of the helicopter—it costs $30,000 to send a recruit through boot camp—when you said I've got what it takes to be a marine, *this* is what it takes—you jump off now or get out of here."

The poor kid is sweating, and his legs are trembling uncontrollably, as if they had just had a heavy charge of electricity pumped through them. "Are you scared of heights?" the tattooed DI asks him. "Yes, sir," says the recruit. An officer comes over to talk to him, and by this time it is clear that the recruit is not going to jump that day; in fact, he is so upset that he can hardly speak.

The technique is to bring anyone who fails to jump back later when there is no one else around. If that doesn't work, there is a closer look at the recruit's record, and often some terrible childhood traumas are revealed. One youth had been held out over a balcony by his stepfather as a form of punishment; in other cases incest, rape, and child abuse were involved. It turns out that as a child this recruit had fallen off a haystack. He was away sick the day he should have done the "slide for life," and he never did manage to jump off Holberton Tower, thus ending his attempt to become a marine.

The tattooed DI, reflecting on all this, says the three most challenging physical things at boot camp are the slide for life, the rappel, and the swim with clothes. One of the curiosities of the rappel is that the DI has seen male recruits occasionally refuse to do it, but never has he known a female recruit to flunk it.

"They're attentive and really motivated," he says. "I remember one girl who cried all the way up the ladder, jumped, and cried all the way down. She came back up again for the second jump, still crying. When she was down she looked back up at me with tears all over her face, shook her fist, and yelled she would never do it again." He pauses, looking down at the sea of male faces below. "Women recruits will do anything."

Females are now fully integrated into the Parris Island training cycle, although they live in separate quarters, have slightly different physical standards to meet, and do not do unarmed combat training such as pugil stick sparring. But they do the three toughest physical tests: the confidence course, rappelling, and swimming. All the corps' enlisted women marines are trained here; San Diego, the West Coast equivalent, only takes male recruits. The dropout rate for women is roughly the same as for men.

A number of things have not—and probably never will—change at Parris Island as long as there is a United States Marine Corps: the style of the place, immaculately neat and tidy, with brisk figures marching purposefully in all directions bent on pressing errands; the special intonation of the marching cadence, which sounds something like "awn-kup-ray-pay-yer-lawf"; the recruits' reflexive shouting "Yes, SIR," "No, SIR," even when no one appears to be asking them anything; the stress on Marine Corps history, valor, and pride; and the delight of the relatives and friends at the final graduation ceremony.

The indoctrination side of marine boot camp—crude and a little childish to the outsider—continues relatively unchanged. Recruits still study the marines' history closely, sing the corps' hymn nightly at horizontal attention on their beds, are fed such old-style Hollywood pap as *The Sands of Iwo Jima* with John Wayne and Jack Webb's *DI* in their squad bays, and are "protected" whenever possible from critical comment in the outside world. A 1987 issue of *Time* magazine, carrying a picture of a marine with a black eye on the cover and dealing with the marine security guard scandal in Moscow, was not stocked by the PX on Parris Island though the magazine was normally sold there.

The physical side of the training is still demanding. The confidence course has its hair-raising moments, the first sight of the rappelling tower is invariably terrifying, and having to swim in deep water with your clothes on is not a cheering thought for someone who can't swim. Also being whacked across the head, albeit in a football helmet, with an eight-pound ash pugil stick is no fun at all.

Recruits still get hurt and occasionally die at boot camp. A young man dropped dead of a heart attack in 1986 at Parris Island; he had a heart defect that, had it been detected, would have kept him out of the Marine Corps. Another recruit suffered a crushed vertebra and had to be discharged when a comrade fell on him while they were on the confidence course. These incidents, however, have demonstrably different causes from the Ribbon Creek and McClure fatalities.

There is little doubt that while boot camp is still tough and a shock for the uninitiated it is no longer as rough, frightening, brutal, or as mindless as it often was. "Everything is very pasteurized at Parris Island these days," says a young training officer. Some people within the Marine Corps say the pendulum has swung too far, and the most vocal of these critics are the DIs themselves.

The debate centers, as it always has, on what is the best way to take a young civilian and turn him into a fighting marine. The most telling criticism comes from the younger DIs, men who were themselves trained under the reforms that came in after the McClure death in 1976 and who are a different, more thoughtful breed than the old groaners of the previous generation.

They are not advocating a return to the brutal methods of the past, but they believe the magic formula that gave them the power and the freedom to turn raw civilian clay into highly motivated, superbly disciplined fighting men has been seriously tampered with, if not removed altogether.

They complain of "micromanagement" by the officers, which diminishes their authority over the recruits and reduces their motivation and self-esteem. They cite great pressure from above to keep the attrition rates low, thus retaining young men who should not be in the Marine Corps and who could jeopardize the lives of their comrades in combat.

They believe these pressures have their origin in the Marine Corps hierarchy in Washington that is trying hard to keep the corps "fat" and is worried by congressional admonitions not to waste men who have been successfully recruited.

They list abuses such as retaining recruits who lie about drug taking and those who blatantly disobey orders. One recruit, according to a senior DI, sat on his footlocker for seven days, refusing to work, and was still not dismissed. Other charges include night marches done in daylight, exam results that have been falsified, good marksmen firing at poor marksmens' targets, and DIs punching holes in targets with a pencil to keep the scores up.

The result, the DIs say, is that although the finished product may look and sound like a marine, a number of them are still civilians at heart and are therefore likely to be unreliable in combat.

"The recruits obey orders," says a DI, "but you're not getting that instant response that you used to. They respond more slowly and sometimes ask questions at the wrong time. Questions are OK, but at the proper time and place, not when you are under fire and the officer or NCO says: 'Take that hill.'"

Another DI is so disillusioned with the system that he is planning to leave the Marine Corps even though he loves recruit training. He says he would go into combat with the new marines, but he fears many would be unnecessarily killed because of what he regards as flawed training.

Many DIs look back with a sense of nostalgia to when the attrition rate used to be 30 or 40 percent; now, according to Marine Corps statistics, it has been hovering between 14 and 18 percent for the last five years. "The Marine Corps has always been

selective—the proud, the few," says another DI. "But now it's a case of many are called and all—or virtually all—are chosen."

Criticism is even more vocal from the older DIs. "Doing away with the motivation platoon was a disaster," says a gunnery sergeant who was a DI at Parris Island in the early 1970s. "It was the best way of showing recruits not to be shitheads. We used to make a big show of it. They'd be crying and all covered with mud in the ditch and then we'd hose them down in front of the whole platoon. It made a big impact on the others."

"You've got to own their minds," says another old-timer. "What's the use of having physically fit bodies if you don't own their minds. The old proven chain of command has broken down. The recruits used to fear the DIs. Now it's the DIs who fear the recruits. These kids will turn and run in combat."

There is criticism of the new DIs, too. "A lot of the DIs who were trained after 1976 don't know any better," remarks a third. "Others are brown-nosers, but I can tell you that 90 percent of the DIs down here are disillusioned."

One DI was taken off the drill field for "assault," which, he says, amounted to nothing more than positioning a recruit in formation and pointing out dirty belt brasses as they hung around a recruit's neck for inspection. In each case, he claims, the recruit had decided to quit and had nothing to lose—and a vindictive pleasure to gain—by reporting him.

"I'm a kind of throwback because I love the Marine Corps," he says. "I used to be in the air force and first saw the marines close-up with their immaculate uniforms, snap and pop when I was stationed in Greece. But lots of kids come in now for the job training. The corps does not become part of them. It's just a job."

Marine Corps officers involved in recruit training vigorously counter these charges. They emphasize the high-profile nature of Marine Corps recruit training, especially at Parris Island, which for many people is shorthand for the Marine Corps itself.

Preceding page
A new marine:
Graduation Day

"There's no outcry in the fleet over a death," says a senior officer, "but if it happens here it ricochets through the halls of Congress."

"Too many of the old-timers are suffering from 'euphoric recall,'" says a major. "Former marines come back and are critical because the recruits are not going through what they went through. If they are honest, they will admit they hated it at the time."

"Somebody has to draw the line," says a general, "and that's our job, not the DIs. The average DI is twenty-five years old, so supervision is vital. Some of them try to push that imaginary line back, and we have to check that tendency."

The charge of excessive micromanagement by officers—becoming involved in the nitty-gritty of the job that should properly be left to the NCOs—runs throughout the Marine Corps, and some officers agree with the NCOs. But not at boot camp. Officers there seem to be unanimous that, given the scandals of the past and the public scrutiny of the present, there has to be an ultrastrict monitoring system, even if it annoys the DIs.

Officers and some NCOs who support the present system stress how much society has changed in recent years and how different the modern recruit is from his predecessors. Nearly all the young men and women joining the marines these days are high school graduates, which according to the hierarchy does not necessarily make them better marines but does show that they have staying power. Better educated and more intelligent, these recruits are also more enquiring, more critical, more independent-minded than earlier marines.

Given the increasingly technical nature of warfare, the Marine Corps needs people who have technical skills or the ability to acquire them. Although the Marine Corps is unique among the armed forces in demanding that everyone goes through boot camp (the officers do an equally rigorous period of basic training at Quantico), fewer than one in four of those who pass through Parris Island and San Diego actually goes into the infantry.

There seems little doubt that the officers, rather than the DIs, truly run boot camp these days, although the latter continue to be the most visible and essential ingredient in recruit training. The imposition of the chain of command has not always been easy. A former assistant series commander, then a lieutenant, tells a story of how it was at Parris Island in the immediate aftermath of the post-McClure reforms.

"One day my series commander, a huge guy who had been a college football player, saw a DI hit a recruit and called him into his office. The DI admitted the charge but explained it was better that way because there would be no permanent blot on the recruit's record. The series commander reminded the DI that touching a recruit was strictly against regulations and then asked him if he would want to be treated the same way for disobedience.

"'Yes, sir,' said the DI crisply.

"The officer stood up, drew back his fist, and slammed the DI into the wall with a mighty punch to the chest.

"'Don't let it happen again, sergeant,' the officer said as the winded DI staggered out of his office. And it didn't."

Quite a few senior officers, as well as some NCOs, have made a 180-degree turn on recruit training. Brought up on the old diet of verbal abuse and physical punishment that seemed to serve the corps well in every war that it fought, including the morass of Vietnam, they now strongly defend the current system.

A senior colonel who went through Parris Island as a recruit in the early 1950s and who returned to command the recruit training regiment in the 1970s put it this way: "Boot camp is tough but fortunately the brutality often associated with it in the past is disappearing. Brutality does not make it tough, only brutal. The stress of becoming a marine remains. A recruit need not give up his dignity to become a marine, and an individual who feels that he must strip a man of that dignity is not much of a leader."

This is a long way from the views of those who always believed that the essence of boot camp was to field strip the recruit of his personality and civilian attitudes and remake him in the age-old image of a United States Marine — a fearless, totally obedient, and highly proficient killer.

A sergeant at the time of the Ribbon Creek incident, this colonel later wrote about how he felt then. "A drill instructor had a platoon of recruit goof-offs and was attempting to instill a little discipline by going through the swamps. A few of the recruits didn't listen and, as a result, they drowned. Now, because of a few shitbirds, we would be required to change boot camp and never be able to instill discipline again."

Today, the colonel believes "unequivocally" that the DI was wrong. And, on the key question of whether modern marines would perform as well as old marines in combat, he says: "You can never be sure, but look at Beirut and Grenada, where half the marines involved had been in the corps for less than a year. They did very well. I fought in Vietnam and I personally would feel totally confident leading these young men in combat."

The controversy will doubtless continue. But two things are clear. First, there will not be a return to the verbal abuse and physical intimidation of earlier times. Second, the jury on the fighting qualities of the new marine will remain out until there is another war to test his mettle.

The Naval Academy: Annapolis, Maryland

Of the three armed service academies, the United States Naval Academy in Annapolis is not the oldest (West Point has that distinction), but it is the most beautiful. It was founded in 1845 on a small headland close to where the Severn River meets Chesapeake Bay. Behind it sits the pretty colonial town of Annapolis, Maryland's capital. At any time of year the academy and town display proportion, elegance, and history engraved in brick, mortar, and stone. In deep winter when they are blanketed in snow, or in high summer when enhanced by bright sunlight, green foliage, and a thousand sailboats dancing on the waters, this quiet corner of Maryland has a special enchantment that only undisturbed and living history can produce.

Yet while the historical harmony between town and academy is well established, once inside the grounds, the academy takes on physical dimensions that dwarf Annapolis's narrow brick streets and its pixie houses. Bancroft Hall, where 4,500 midshipmen live and eat, covers several acres and qualifies as one of the world's largest dwellings. There is a 3,500-square-foot multifunction oceanography laboratory and a sports complex with *two* Olympic-size swimming pools.

The place is strewn with historical artifacts: guns, fine naval prints, the flag hoisted by Commodore Perry at the battle of Lake Erie, the table from the mess deck of the battleship U.S.S. *Missouri* on which the Japanese surrender was signed in 1945, and personal items belonging to American naval heroes such as Stephen Decatur, David Glasgow Farragut, George Dewey, and William Frederick Halsey. And in the crypt of the academy's Wren-style chapel lie the remains of John Paul Jones, the patron saint of the U.S. Navy.

Although its functional role is modest, the Naval Academy is a rather special place for the Marine Corps. Slightly under 17 percent of the academy's annual crop of graduates go to the Marine Corps, representing about 10 percent of the corps' total officer strength. The marines' teaching and representational presence amounts to a small detachment of officers and enlisted personnel, headed by a colonel. But in the academy's vast and splendid Memorial Hall, where official ceremonies and receptions are held, there are two reminders of the marines among the navy's pantheon of heroes.

One is an oil painting of the corps' most famous and revered commandant, Major General John A. Lejeune, himself an academy graduate, looking somewhat out of place in his khaki uniform among the admirals' blue and white. The other is a more recent addition. This is a diorama in a glass case, a three-dimensional model depicting Colonel John W. Ripley swinging hand over hand as he placed the charges that blew up the Dong Ha bridge in Vietnam and delayed the North Vietnamese army's advance during the 1972 Easter offensive. A U.S. Marine Corps adviser to the South Vietnamese marines, Ripley was under intense enemy fire as he went back and forth across the bridge with demolitions and fuses. For this feat, he won the Navy Cross, the nation's second highest award for valor. He, too, was an academy graduate who later returned as senior marine here.

The Marine Corps remains physically and psychologically attached to the navy, with whom it has fought side by side ever since the Revolutionary War. The corps, although enjoying a certain autonomy, is administered by the Department of the Navy and answers to its secretary. While the Naval Academy has tradition and cachet, its graduates may turn out to be no better than other marine officers who have entered through less demanding channels. They used to do rather well or rather badly when they joined the corps. But in recent years their performance has been disappointing, at least during the initial phase of their Marine Corps training. Since the academy began commissioning marine officers in 1883, it has provided seven out of twenty-one Marine Corps commandants.

The marine staff at the naval academy, while not on an active recruiting exercise — there are more applicants than they can take — get their point across by their presence and example. Only heavy hitters are sent down to Annapolis from headquarters, whether it is to teach history and English or to show uncoordinated midshipmen how to march. And then, each year, an evening is set aside for midshipmen, who are thinking of "going marine," to have a look at what the corps has to offer.

First there is a general briefing by two captains who do a kind of "network news" routine, punctuating facts with humor. "The Marine Corps today possesses about 9 percent of the uniformed forces in the United States, 11 percent of the various fighter/ attack aircraft, 11 percent of our general purpose divisions, and the nation's only

organic combined arms force," says the captain at the right-hand lectern. "Our corps has grown from its minimum strength of 312 in 1794 to its maximum strength of 522,777 in 1945. The Marine Corps now consists of approximately 198,000 men and women; of this 20,000 are officers and 178,000 enlisted."

He nods to his partner. "Happy are those who chose the corps and said goodbye to boredom forevermore," begins the captain at the other lectern.

After the opening briefing, the young midshipmen wander from room to room listening to and questioning marine officers about the different "military occupational specialties" (MOSs).

"Think infantry," says a major who wears Vietnam campaign medals. It seems a little strange that a midshipman at the Naval Academy, where 70 percent of the curriculum is science and engineering, would want to become a marine infantryman. But, says an officer, "Jumping into the soup is cool with some midshipmen." Quite a few of them are also attracted by the idea of becoming pilots and flying close support for ground troops, something they are less likely to do if they were pilots in the navy.

What would happen to them after graduating from the Naval Academy is explained in some detail. The bad news is that they go back to school, The Basic School in Quantico that all marine officers have to attend. The good news is—or at least used to be—that they did not have to go through Officer Candidates School, the grueling equivalent to the enlisted marine's boot camp. A new commandant, figuring that while the Naval Academy graduates' minds might have been sufficiently stretched in Annapolis, their bodies and souls had gotten off lightly, abruptly changed the rules.

"You'll know more than the others at Quantico," warns a marine officer surrounded by a group of curious midshipmen. "But they'll be a lot hungrier than you."

This year the brigade commander, the top midshipman in the graduating class, has chosen the Marine Corps. He says he was strongly influenced by the quality of the marine officers at the academy. He had considered the Seals, the navy's crack special force, but finally felt he would fit best in the marines' infantry. He will be getting married three days after graduation—in his Marine Corps dress white uniform.

Officers and Others: Quantico, Virginia

OFFICER TRAINING

For every enlisted marine who will never forget his drill instructor and the appearance, smells, and horrors of boot camp, there is an officer whose memories of his painful induction into the Marine Corps at Officer Candidates School in the woods of Quantico, in northern Virginia, may be even more vivid.

OCS, as every marine calls it, endures for the same ten-week period as the enlisted men's boot camp, but it is, by all accounts, tougher.

William Broyles, who went through it in the late sixties, later reproduced the panic—and the language—of the initiation in an *Esquire* article:

There were six showers and forty of us. We scrambled naked over one another, punching and kicking.

"You got ten seconds to get back in the squad bay," the DI yelled. "Any motherfucker not in front of his rack in the position of attention, I am gonna unscrew his head and shit in it!"

We piled out of the showers.

"You assholes don't look clean to me! I won't have any smelly, dirty maggots in my nice clean squad bay. Back to the showers!"

We fought one another to get wet. Someone got a bloody lip. Someone else cut his hand on the shower handle.

"Blood in my showers! You sloppy bunch of shits! Get your toothbrushes! You got ten seconds to be on your hands and knees and clean this fucking head!"

We raced back into the squad bay, tore through our gear, and slipped and fell back into the bathroom, where we scrubbed the floor with our toothbrushes. For two or three hours we stampeded back and forth.

"Move! Move! Move! You don't move, maggots, you gonna fuckin' die!"

It was almost 4:00 in the morning when the lights finally went out.

"On my command: ready—sleep!"

At 5:30 the lights flicked on again. The drill instructors were beating trash cans with broom handles and screaming. We jumped out of bed and for half an hour did brutal calisthenics until we couldn't raise ourselves off the floor. Several men threw up. Others urinated in their underwear and for their sins had to stick their heads in the toilet bowls. The rest of us marched off in the dark to our first breakfast as Marines.

OCS, like boot camp, has cleaned up its language. But it is still a grueling course. The idea behind it is that a marine officer has got to be able to do all that his men can do—and then a bit more. The official attrition rate is twice as high as boot camp (30 percent as compared to 14 percent); the unofficial (i.e. probably more accurate) rate is even higher, sometimes rising to 50 percent, according to instructors on the OCS staff.

The initial physical screening weeds out a lot of candidates, and then injuries take their toll. But it is the mentally irresolute who mainly fall by the wayside once the course is under way. "We don't want all of them here," says a stocky captain whose father was a truck driver and whose mother worked all her life. "They've got to want to be a marine officer real bad to make it through OCS."

There is no secret formula for success, he adds. If a young man is physically fit and has the right mental attitude, he'll make it. That also goes for women, who do the same training as the men with modified physical test requirements. The key is not the size of the chest expansion or the bicep measurement but that old-fashioned commodity that has taken fighting men into battle since time immemorial. Guts.

Officer candidates are trained by the best NCOs the Marine Corps can provide and by hand-picked officers. The course, while similar in many respects to the boot camp syllabus, has some additional distractions. For instance, there is the physical readiness test, which involves a twenty-foot rope climb, push-ups and sit-ups, a fire-man's carry (which means throwing someone roughly your own weight and height over your shoulder and running two hundred yards), fire and maneuver exercises that involve crawling, a three-mile run, and zigzagging, rolling, and firing a rifle over rough terrain.

There is also the reaction course in which candidates take turns leading a group over obstacles that, on the face of it, seem easy but turn out to be the opposite. These are classic officer-training games such as getting a squad over a notional river with two planks, a barrel, and a piece of rope. "Oh, and by the way," the instructor adds as the eager candidate begins to organize his men, "don't forget to take this box of 'medical supplies.'"

And then there is the combat course, which is different from the obstacle course. Three quarters of a mile long, the combat course is set in the woods. It simulates likely conditions on a battlefield and includes a number of rope or wire crossings of actual streams that the participant must negotiate by walking, sliding, or pulling himself along by his arms. There are walls and a hill to scale by means of dangling ropes, barbed wire to crawl under, ditches, and a nasty drainage pipe to scramble through.

When it has been raining the drainage pipe fills up with muddy water and you have to swim or heave yourself through it virtually submerged. The course has to be performed tactically—that is, in web gear, helmet, and rifle; candidates must run, crawl, and crouch between obstacles. The final objective, the easiest in the exercise though the hardest in real life, is the notional enemy bunker at the end of the course.

This is demolished by the exhausted but triumphant candidates with notional grenades and a lot of murderous yelling.

Once through Officer Candidates School, the newly commissioned marine second lieutenant goes on to The Basic School and by now well versed in military acronymese will simply call it "TBS." Situated at Camp Barrett, on another part of Quantico's sprawling terrain, TBS is housed in a notably uncharismatic cluster of buildings. Put up in the 1950s, the complex looks more like a motel or a trade school than a military academy.

A group of Naval Reserve Officer Training Corps college students are in for a couple of days to look around, listen, fire a few weapons, and see if the Marine Corps might suit them. A marine major, of medium height and endowed with a Tarzan chest, strides into the briefing room.

"Attention on deck!" shouts one of the TBS staff, and the students, all in camouflage utilities, jump to their feet. "Sit down, please," says the major going over to the lectern.

With the help of slides and a prepared brief, he explains the school's purpose and outlines its curriculum.

"The Basic School is unique in the sense that no other armed service has a formal school equivalent to it. Every marine officer, regardless of sex, source of commission, or potential assignment, begins his or her life at The Basic School. First established in 1891 at Marine Barracks, Washington, D.C., The Basic School has been home-ported in Annapolis, Parris Island, Norfolk, Philadelphia, and various camps at Quantico. Approximately fifteen hundred officers from various commissioning sources attend The Basic School each year . . . [including] between fifty and eighty women officers, who undergo the same course of instruction as male officers with minor modifications to conform with the law and basic physiological differences. But the objective is a constant: to reach the top."

The course lasts twenty-three weeks and covers three main subjects: leadership, which is taught largely through each student filling leadership roles among his or her peers; academic instruction, consisting of tactics and command and leadership training that include firing and care of the basic infantry weapons; and military skills such as marksmanship, land navigation, and physical fitness. The young officers also do amphibious exercises, attend mess nights and official receptions, and plunder their savings or credit lines for the three thousand dollars needed to pay for their dress blues and sea bag of required uniforms.

"The Basic School's mission," sums up the major, "has at its heart a single purpose—to prepare newly commissioned officers to lead our most precious asset: the enlisted marine."

After TBS, officers pursue their military occupational specialty. Potential aviators go to the navy's flight school in Pensacola, Florida; artillery officers go to the army's field artillery school in Fort Sill, Oklahoma; and tracked vehicle officers go to the armor school in Fort Knox, Kentucky. But infantry officers remain at Quantico to do a specialized infantry course, a further nine weeks of study and tests.

Even when a marine officer finally shakes the reddish earth of Quantico's pine- and birch-covered training areas off his boots, he hopes he will be back before long. If he is successful, the Amphibious Warfare School awaits him when he has reached the rank of captain, and the Command and Staff College is ready to continue his education when he becomes a major. It is not surprising that Quantico is known as the "crossroads of the Marine Corps."

The results of all this can be clearly seen in the fleet and wherever you come across young marine officers. They are a confident breed, very pumped up. Quantico has given them a new middle initial: L for Leadership. Reflecting on the officer corps, a seasoned lieutenant colonel who began his career as an enlisted man, did two tours in Vietnam, and served with Britain's Royal Marines, commented:

"I think the leadership of the officers in the Marine Corps is probably the best in the world. We have a very hands-on leadership approach—we participate, we play, we show sincerity and interest, and I think we are competent. That's hard to resist."

This officer agreed, though, that marine officers are often guilty of micromanaging, of trying to do the NCOs job as well as their own. Young officers are told that their predecessors learned as much, and probably more, from their first platoon sergeant than they did at Quantico and that it is a good idea to continue the tradition. But NCOs will tell you that that does not happen as much it should. They often criticize the younger officers for being *overtrained*, a state of affairs that, in their view, does not make up for a second lieutenant's lack of experience in the field.

"We try to push them into relying on good staff NCOs," says the TBS briefing major. "But some company commanders believe in 'officer-run companies' and the result is that we waste years of NCO experience."

It is 6:15 A.M. on a crisp spring morning. There is a sense of expectation in the air as every tree and shrub seems ready to burst into bloom. There is also expectation among the two hundred and thirty second lieutenants gathering in front of TBS headquarters for a twenty-five-mile hike. They are "tactically" accoutered: helmets, rifles, flak vests, and packs; extra weight in the form of platoon weapons such as machine guns, mortars, grenade launchers, and radios is shared. The average load is seventy-two pounds, plus the platoon gear that is passed around.

There is a lot of laughing and bantering as they line up. They have already done two ten-mile and fifteen-mile marches during their training, working up to this marathon-length test of endurance. Do they enjoy it?

"They're trying to fool themselves that they do," says a captain on the TBS staff. "They're pumping themselves up, but soon it'll be tough mental work: left foot in front of right and right foot in front of left."

With the women in the lead, they set off at a brisk pace. The march will take about eight hours. They will stop every hour for a ten-minute break to drink water, change socks, and chew on dry rations. Plumes of warm breath float upward as the column swings and sways down a long, empty road. One group breaks into a cadence: "I bumped my head upon her toe. She said 'Marine, you're far too low.'" One young man is carrying a ghetto-blaster radio, another has a yo-yo in his hand, and a woman is sucking a lollipop. "Want to join us?" shouts another, spitting out a stream of tobacco juice.

11:40 A.M. The column has covered about eighteen miles now and is trudging along a gravel road in the woods. A sturdy group near the rear is still calling cadence, but some of the young officers are showing signs of stress. A few have taken their helmets off, one young woman is holding another's hand, there is some cursing among the men, and the ghetto-blaster has disappeared. (Or its owner may be in the truck that is slowly creeping along in the rear and has collected a handful of casualties.) The tobacco chewer is as jaunty as ever. "Want to join us?" he sings out again.

Quantico entered into Marine Corps history in 1917 when thousands of marines were trained here for the bloody killing grounds of France in World War I. It has grown greatly since and is the home of a number of specialist organizations in addition to being the crucible of the officer corps. There is the Staff NCO Academy, run entirely by staff NCOs, the Marine Security Guard Battalion that trains marines for embassy duty around the world, and the Marine Helicopter Squadron One, an experimental unit that tests new helicopter techniques but also, more visibly, provides transportation for the President and visiting heads of state.

Marine Corps doctrine and development is handled at Quantico; *Leatherneck,* the most popular marine magazine at the enlisted level, and the Marine Corps *Gazette,* a magazine used principally by officers as a forum, are produced on the base by the Marine Corps Association; and there is a fine air and ground museum. The FBI Academy is also here. It has no formal links with the corps, but since many marines join the FBI after they leave, there is a symbiotic connection.

Quantico town, surrounded and vastly outnumbered by the marine base, retains the charm of an earlier, less complicated era. The officer caste is reflected in the tailors' and haberdashers' stores, old and new. The occasional good bar, encrusted with marine memorabilia, lacks the sleaze associated with the giant marine bases at Camp Lejeune, North Carolina; Camp Pendleton, California; and Camp Hansen, Okinawa.

MARINE SNIPERS

A smart commander makes maximum use of all his assets in a fight. All infantry commanders must be strongly versed in the employment of snipers and employ them effectively and correctly in all forms of tactical training. The classical sniper definitely has an application on the modern battlefield and if utilized correctly will greatly contribute to our quest of winning the first battle of the next war. [From the U.S. Marine Corps manual on sniping]

On paper Colonel David J. Willis, commanding officer of the Weapons Training Battalion at Quantico, sounds like a pretty ordinary marine in charge of a pretty ordinary unit. But appearances can be deceptive, even in the Marine Corps, where people tend to look alike, talk alike, and act alike. Willis's innocuous-sounding command cloaks functions at the heart of the Marine Corps as well as at its cutting edge: marksmanship and sniping.

Quantico is the home of the marines competitive shooting and special weapons training. It is here that the best shots in the corps congregate and compete with the old M-14 rifle, and it is here that marines and many others are trained in such esoterica as concealed weaponry. A navy admiral, an air force colonel, an army captain, indeed any Defense Department individual deemed to be in a "high risk" category could receive special weapons training here.

But it is sniping, one of the oldest and deadliest forms of warfare, that gives the place a special aura. Marine Corps scout-sniper instructors are trained at Quantico and then go out to the Fleet Marine Forces to pass on their skills. Navy Seals, FBI agents, and other operatives in the twilight world of long-range killing are also trained by marine experts.

It takes two months to train a scout-sniper instructor. The first month is largely devoted to markmanship and the second to camouflage and concealment, individual movement and stalking, and range estimation. To qualify as a sniper, the student must have an 80 percent success rate in hitting a stationary man-sized target at one thousand yards and a moving target at eight hundred yards.

The second month is as critical as the first. A sniper can be the best shot in the world, but he will be worthless if he cannot approach his target undetected and accurately estimate its range. Three groups of twenty-four scout-sniper instructors are trained every year at Quantico and the attrition rate is between 25 and 40 percent.

Marine snipers operate in two-man teams. One is the actual sniper, the other the observer, who is also a qualified sniper. The sniper carries binoculars, a small tripod, two boxes of ammunition, a .45-caliber pistol, and the M-40A1 sniper rifle, which was developed by the marines themselves and is a vast improvement on the Remington M-40 used in Vietnam.

The observer carries the standard M-16A2 marine infantry rifle, a radio, and the twenty-power M-49 scope. The scope is used primarily to make wind adjustments for the sniper to get him on target. The observer can also track the bullet through the scope because the projectile displaces air that creates a "wake," rather like that of a boat. If the sniper misses with his first shot, the observer can make a quick correction that will help a second attempt.

Quantico has sixty thousand acres of land and some of the best ranges in the world. Out in the woods, a couple of sergeants explain the art of sniping. Both men are dressed in ghillie suits, a disguise inspired by the Scottish gamekeeper, which they make themselves. One of them has made his suit out of rope and string and looks a bit

Officer Candidates School (OCS), the officer equivalent of enlisted marines' boot camp: Quantico

like a mangy lion, though when he gets down in the dry winter underbrush he virtually disappears.

"The hardest thing to do," he says, "is to relax, to be patient, to move, if necessary, at an inch at a time. The ghillie suit protects you from quite a lot of insects. The others get in and live with you. What you try to do is redirect your irritability, turning it into hate and contempt for the enemy."

The most dangerous opponent is not snakes, which if left alone will rarely attack, but dogs. FBI tracker dogs are brought in as part of the course, and snipers sometimes go to extraordinary lengths to evade them. Colonel Willis tells of the sniper who took off all his clothes, climbed a tree and "wearing nothing but a smile" sat there clutching his rifle. But the dog found him. His embarrassment was complete when he looked down and saw that the handler was a woman.

Back in the battalion headquarters, a lieutenant colonel elaborates on the qualities needed to be a sniper. "It requires qualities quite different from those associated with reconnaissance, another elite activity in the Marine Corps," he says. "Recon training is very aggressive, very action oriented. With sniping, everything is deliberate, slow, and calculated. Sniping is a highly personal form of warfare. You can never tell who is going to be good at it by appearances. Take Carlos Hathcock, for example. He was the marines' ace sniper in Vietnam with ninety-three confirmed kills. But he was—and is—a quiet and mild sort of guy."

In the background, there is the whine of a high-speed drill and some serious grinding sounds coming from the armorer's shop. The marines build their own competition and sniper rifles. The former is an adaptation of the old M-14 rifle with a heavier barrel and a bolt instead of an automatic action. The sniper rifle is a sleek-looking weapon with a camouflaged fiberglass stock that doesn't break or warp like its wooden predecessor, a long smooth stainless steel barrel, and a ten-power scope made specially for the Marine Corps by John Unertl in Pittsburgh. Marine snipers do not use night scopes. The Unertl picks up 93 percent of ambient light at night (that is, starlight and moonlight) and that apparently is enough for a sniper to hit a target at three hundred yards. Only highly qualified marine gunsmiths are allowed to remove these scopes. Each rifle weighs more than thirteen pounds and needs, as the saying goes, a "big left arm" to fire it effectively.

Colonel David Willis's office at Quantico is like no other in the Marine Corps. It is large, light, and crammed with memorabilia. There are shooting trophies, old photographs, pictures and statues of John Wayne, a clock with enlisted men's rank insignia instead of numbers (1:00 is a private first class; 11:00, a sergeant major), and a bright red Hudson Bay blanket coat given to the colonel by John Riggins, the former Washington Redskins' hard-charging running back. There is a long conference table with jars of peanuts, jellybeans, and candy on it for whoever drops by. On the colonel's desk sits his marksman's campaign cover (the Smokey the Bear hat worn only by boot camp drill instructors and shooting team members). The hat, made by John B. Stetson and Company, is rimed with with salt and sweat. "I'd wear it to bed," says the colonel, "if it didn't wrinkle up."

Colonel Willis is a distinguished marksman, the winner of thirteen gold medals. But he is also distinguished by his longevity in his present job—he has been here for more than a decade—and his pivotal role as "Mr. Marksman-Sniper" of the Marine Corps. With his shaven head, sunken gray eyes, and soft voice, he epitomizes the sniper's low-keyed approach. He is laid back rather than flamboyant, humorous rather than menacing, spectral rather than physical. But he leaves no doubt that his passion is his trade and that his trade is dispatching the enemy, one-on-one, in the most efficient and summary fashion.

"Snipers are something that people like to read about," the colonel says, tucking a plug of tobacco into the side of his mouth and pouring himself a cup of black coffee. "They sound fascinating, intriguing, and instill fear in the heart of man. But, to us, the

scout-sniper is a supporting arm, two per company, eight per battalion, and seventy-two per division.

"The kind of individual who does well at this is one who has a lot of common sense, is methodical, who thinks before he acts. People with hunting and fishing in their background tend to do well. If there's one key word in the whole thing, it's patience."

Does the sniper have to have a killer instinct?

The colonel leans over and fires a burst of tobacco juice into a brass spittoon.

"I think it's part of what all marines know they have to do," he says slowly. "If he follows his training he will be successful."

Could he misuse his skills?

"Most of our combat skills count on bringing up the level of the adrenalin in order to excel," says the colonel. "But the sniper is different. He is an individual who can best do his job if he is patient, if he can control his heartbeat. He should bring his heartbeat down as low as he can. A lot of men can bring their adrenalin up. We don't want that. The sniper has to get to the objective and back again. He also has got to record in his mind what he sees and be able to bring it back and tell a commander what he has seen. He's got to understand camouflage and concealment. We don't teach him anything that is wild and woolly, just the ability to deliver a shot over a longer length of terrain than the normal marine infantryman would cover."

What did he learn from Vietnam?

"We weren't as good at our cover and concealment as we could be. Then there have been awesome changes in the gun. We've changed from a wood to a fiberglass stock because wood warps and breaks, although I know there is a great romanticism attached to wooden stocks. Once fiberglass is seated, it's good for all eternity. We also have a new barrel and scope so the gun supports the man; ten out of ten, the gun will outshoot the man. That's the way it should be.

Colonel David
J. Willis and the
M-40A1 sniper rifle
with its Unertl scope
Overleaf
Officers' mess
night: Quantico

"A lot of the course here is designed to make the students irritable," Willis continues. "It's long hours, six days a week, up at 4:30 A.M and we work them until nine, ten, some days until midnight, and in-between they have got to study. It's designed that way because if a man is getting a regular amount of sleep, you'll see one side of him. But as an individual loses sleep and you keep pushing him, you'll see another side of him. Then you find out who really wants to be here and who doesn't. What we want to know is what is behind his eyes, what is different about him. A lot of the time I'll have marines coming in here and saying: 'I can't do this. I don't like moving one inch at a time. I need to get back to the regular infantry.'

"Those who make it don't wear insignia like the scuba badge or jump wings. They're not hit men. Good snipers will want to be fed and watered, but they'll go anywhere. It's frightening how good they can be. What they learn here they learn for a lifetime. It's in the mind."

Marine snipers are taught to expect only one chance at the target, though other services have a more generous philosophy. "I think history proves that you're only going to get one shot," Willis says.

Talking of other weapons, the colonel mentions pistols. "People don't realize that pistols are defensive weapons. Any pistol ever made—and I'm not being sarcastic or funny—is a defensive weapon. If you're attacking with a pistol, you've probably been smoking something that ain't authorized. You'll be in deep trouble, and you'd better spend your time bringing all supporting arms to bear."

A gunnery sergeant, who has been working on a sniper scope, comes in. He has a chat with Willis and scoops up a handful of jelly beans on his way out. There is an easy cameraderie between the colonel and his men that is reminiscent of the marine aviators.

Willis looks around at the faded photographs of old shooting champions. "My wife has never seen me shoot though I've won virtually every competition there is. She hates sweat and violence. It's strange." He pauses and grins as if considering the thought for the first time. "Sweat and violence are the only things I like."

In terms of cold mechanical logic,
the United States does not need a Marine Corps.
However, for good reasons that completely transcend cold logic,
the United States *wants* a Marine Corps.

FROM *FIRST TO FIGHT* BY VICTOR H. KRULAK

PART 2:
IN THE
FLEET

Overleaf
Evening colors
performed by
the marine detachment
on the fantail
of the battleship
U.S.S. *Missouri,* the
ship on which
the Japanese surrender
was signed in 1945.
Long Beach, California

Norway

FORT MCCOY, WISCONSIN

It is early evening and gathered in the theater of this old World War II army camp are about two hundred marines, listening to a briefing by their regimental commander. Tomorrow they will fly to Norway for Exercise Cold Winter. "A lot of people say marines can't hack it in cold weather, that we are a lot of little pussies," says the colonel, a Central Casting marine who is short, has graying, close-cropped hair, and, more often than not, has a cigar clamped in the corner of his mouth.

He paces the stage. "But we're not," he barks. "When we get to Norway I want you all to reach down into your sea bags, grab your nuts, and strap them on. There's no rear in this exercise, and the British will be sure to infiltrate. They always do." He pauses. "Would we ever do such a thing?"

"Shit, yes!" comes a voice from the back row.

The colonel permits himself a tight smile. He goes on to tell his audience to watch out for avalanches, noting changes in the weather and such signs as twisted telephone poles. (Last year an avalanche killed sixteen Norwegian soldiers, and Exercise Cold Winter was cancelled). The marines should also be on the alert for snooping Russian observers, who may be accompanied by Norwegian escorts.

"Answer their questions directly," the colonel says. "Tell them what you're doing. There's nothing classified. Be proud—the eyes of the world will be upon you. And when I see the pictures," he adds, echoing a concern of military commanders that reaches back to the Romans, "I want to see everyone wearing the same uniform."

He pauses again and raises a square hand. "Remember the old motto of the Marine Raiders: Gung Ho. It means 'pull together,' and that's what we've got to do. We'll be surrounded and outnumbered. But that's nothing new to the Marine Corps. It just means we don't have so far to go to get 'em. Good luck."

It seems an unlikely scenario for U.S. Marines, but in a few hours four thousand of them will be heading for northern Norway. During the last decade the marines have trained with allied forces well above the Arctic Circle in one of the coldest spots in the world. The deployment is part of the marines' role in helping to defend Europe's flanks in the event of a Soviet attack. In this sector, however, there would be no storming of the beaches. The plan is to insert winter-trained forces into northern Norway, before hostilities begin, to deter Soviet aggression or to halt an invasion should one later occur. A marine brigade, flown into friendly airfields, would join British and Dutch forces to stiffen the Norwegian army's defenses. Heavy equipment, supplies, and artillery—prepositioned in caves in central Norway—would, according to the plan, sustain the marines for thirty days, by which time seaborne supplies could be brought in.

Exercise Cold Winter this year does not involve a whole brigade. But enough men and equipment, including amphibious tractors, fast-moving armored troop carriers, special snow vehicles, helicopters, F/A 18 Hornet fighters, and Hercules air-to-air refueling aircraft, are going to make the war game as realistic as possible. The exercise has the U.S. Marines uncharacteristically on the defensive, defending the key airfield at Evenes (pronounced "Everness"), helped by a British parachute battalion and elements of the Norwegian army. The "enemy" consists of the British Royal Marines, the Dutch Marines, and Norwegian armor. Since the three different marine forces all are on the friendliest of terms and share regular exchange programs, and the Norwegians are among the most loyal and obliging of America's NATO allies, it sounds like a lot of fun, if a little unreal.

However, briefing officers assure you that everyone takes it seriously once the five-day exercise is underway. It even gets a bit physical at times when opposing forces meet head on and the umpires (or "controllers," as they prefer to be called) are out of sight. The British paras are particularly fond of a shakedown, preferably with their old rivals, the Royal Marines, and pitting the two against each other in this particular exercise is bound to provide an opportunity.

But beyond the friendly rivalry there is a deadly enemy who threatens all on this venture. He is "General Winter." "When the windchill factor is −55°F, you can die within minutes if you don't do the right things," says a battalion commander. "You need 4,500 calories and up to five quarts of water a day. Frostbite and hypothermia are dangerous but dehydration is the real killer. You don't think about drinking lots of water in the arctic, and that's one reason why cold-weather fighting is more demanding than jungle warfare. Squad leaders are instructed to force the men to drink if necessary and to watch their eyes for signs of lassitude. Survival in these conditions requires a sustained individual effort. It's mental as much as physical."

It's also a good idea not to fall into a Norwegian fjord without protective clothing on. A couple of minutes in that kind of water is enough to finish off most people. There's also an increased risk of accidents on the icy, windswept terrain, quite apart from the periodic avalanches that took their tragic toll the previous year. Six months earlier in another part of Norway, twelve marines died in a helicopter accident, and another was killed when an amphibious vehicle ran over him. Narrow, winding icy roads of compacted snow pose additional hazards for drivers more accustomed to the heat-baked blacktops of North Carolina and southern California.

Cold Winter is important to the marines for a number of reasons: it tests the air-landed capability of the thirteen-thousand-strong marine brigade; it hones cold-weather training already done in the United States (especially movement across inhospitable terrain on skis and snowshoes); it provides invaluable experience in infantry tactics and combined arms operations; it highlights the problems of working with foreign forces; and it makes an important political point—to NATO allies and to the Pentagon hierarchy alike—that the U.S. Marines have a role to play in Europe, a theater they haven't appeared in since the epic battles on the western front in World War I.

The big question mark hanging over all this is whether the marines and other U.S. forces would be able to get to this vital sector, which has a common border with the Soviet Union and whose airfields and fjords command the North Atlantic, in time. It would take about two hundred and fifty air sorties to move the brigade from the United States to Norway. But that can only be answered, as all war games are eventually answered, by war itself. Meanwhile, the games go on.

Fort McCoy, Wisconsin, an old Indian-fighting base known as Camp McCoy, grew up in World War II when it trained thousands of men for combat in distant lands. The famous Nisei Battalion, composed of Japanese and Hawaiian Americans who won more decorations than any other American unit, prepared itself here. The father of a marine major on the current exercise was here then and still insists, his son says, on calling it *Camp* McCoy. The nearest town is called Sparta, not inappropriately, and the base itself is now used mainly by the National Guard. The buildings, designed to last the duration of the war, remain here forty years later. Patched, worn, and nostalgic, like old soldiers, they live on. In one of them a battalion commander is having a final briefing with his company officers and sergeant major.

"The Royal Marines are the best there is in cold-weather warfare," he says, "and they'll be better than us on skis. But they rarely change their tactics. They like to leapfrog and use their rigid raiders (small hardshell boats) for the amphibious hook. They did it in the Falklands War, and they'll do it in Norway. They completely disagree with our use of helicopters to lift troops. Most of their movement is done over land or by water. What we must do is keep on the move, too, try to take the initiative, and make them stop and think."

The battalion executive officer lists the strengths, dispositions, and missions of friendly and enemy forces. The former are significantly outnumbered. "Sounds just about even," says a captain, drawing a laugh all around.

At the end of the row of chairs sits a young second lieutenant who flew up from Quantico in Virginia the night before to join his new battalion and to command the heavy-weapons platoon. He has just graduated and decided to forgo his leave. "It speaks poorly of his judgment," says the battalion commander with a smile, "but well of his enthusiasm."

The rifle companies will be spread out, acting largely independently much of the time. Most of the action will be at night, with the troops resting up during the day in chilly foxholes dug in the snow. The young captains describe their plans and debate tactics.

They seem confident and totally engaged, aware perhaps that this may well be their moment of glory in the Marine Corps. No longer wet behind the ears, as young lieutenants tend to be, but still close to the ground, they are in command of their men on the cutting edge of the corps. There is no better command, old marines will tell you, than leading a rifle company in the field. As a group, they are cheerful, cocky, and iconoclastic. Bureaucracy, politics, inertia, and perhaps disillusionment will come later. Right now they are having a ball.

Wrapping it up, the battalion sergeant major, a black veteran of Vietnam and many years in a changing Marine Corps, sounds a word of caution. "The men are declimatized because of the unusually mild weather here, and morale is a bit low due to the end of the training cycle. We need to spread the information downward, explain why there have been delays, why they are going backward and forward." He pauses and looks around at his youthful audience. "They also want to kick ass and get on with it. And they want to see some Norwegian women."

Down the road from Fort McCoy is Volk airfield, now used mainly by the Air National Guard. It's midnight, and tonight more than four hundred marines are crowded into the heated hangars—waiting, waiting, waiting. They have been here for almost twelve hours but there is no apparent frustration; instead they seem to have taken up residence like an occupying army in an almost cozy way. Some are cocooned in their equipment, heads on rolled sleeping bags, feet on packs, their weapons clustered in casual heaps. Others are kicking a ball, playing dominoes or cards, or listening to music on "ghetto-blaster" radios.

One of the senior officers who is organizing the task of shifting four thousand marines, their equipment, weapons, ammunition, and food to Norway, more than three thousand miles away, takes a break to recount a drama that happened at Volk Field a few days earlier. The pilot of a small plane died of a heart attack in flight, leaving in charge a very frightened passenger who had never driven anything larger or more airborne than a small car. Marine air controllers began to talk him down with simplified instructions and reassuring phrases: "Remember, Ralph," they said soothingly, "altitude is our friend."

Eventually, they got him over the runway. But just as he was about to land he opened the throttle instead of closing it, bounced mightily, and took off again. In the confusion, he dropped his microphone and went off the air. Fortunately, he could still hear the marines and finally made a safe landing, swearing he would never go aloft again unless there were fifteen pilots aboard.

The officer telling this story has a fatherly attitude toward everyone in the unit, from the commanding general on down to the youngest private. "They're amazingly patient, aren't they?" he says, pointing to the camouflage green mounds of marines strewn around the hangar. As he talks, he takes out his Zippo lighter and burns an errant thread off his immaculate utility uniform. An old infantryman.

At last the aircraft is ready. It is a chartered Boeing 747 of Flying Tigers, whose colorful and checkered career began in China before World War II. The marines, some already wearing their thermal "Mickey Mouse" boots, file on board. An enormously

Overleaf
F/A 18 Hornet fighter refueling over Norway

heavy safe, which was chained to a supporting column in the Fort McCoy headquarters and which contains the unit's documents (and petty cash?), is dragged on board and disappears into the rear of the aircraft.

A reserve major appears on the upper deck. Here the senior officers — and your scribe, who has already acquired a nickname, "Soupe du Jour" — are packed like sardines in first-class ambience but steerage-style seating.

"Aha, the usual suspects!" he cries.

"Sit down, counselor," comes a voice used to giving orders.

"Yes, *sir*," replies the Washington tax lawyer who not so many hours ago was in a three-piece suit advising clients on Capitol Hill.

The intercom crackles with the throaty vocals of a powerfully built blonde flight attendant. "If there is anyone not going to Norway," she breathes, "now would be a good time to disembark. Fasten your seatbelts, extinguish all cigarettes, and" (pause) "stow your weapons under your seats, butts toward the aisle."

THE ARCTIC

Situated on a tongue of land bounded by deep fjords, the airfield at Evenes from above looks like the deck of an aircraft carrier. Chartered Boeing 747s and U.S. Air Force C-141's (one of them with a female copilot) deliver a steady stream of marines to this snowbound land. Standing in the bright sunlight, at first it does not seem that cold. But after fifteen minutes or so the extremities begin to numb, and it is time to clamber into long johns, nylon Goretex parkas, and heavily insulated thermal snow boots in which your feet sweat rather than freeze.

It is a majestic part of the world, this northern cone of Europe with its snow-covered mountains and valleys, sparkling in the winter sun; its clumps of fir, spruce, and pine; and its gray-blue fjords that *feel* as deep as the map says they are. It is a place of military history, too, with the port of Narvik at the head of the Ofot Fjord, due east of Evenes, and easily accessible by land and water. It was there that one of the great early sea battles of World War II was fought between the British and German navies. Half a dozen German fighting ships still lie in the icy waters at the bottom of Narvik harbor.

That war also lives on in the minds of Norwegians, who tend to be anguished over their country's quick capitulation, proud of its later resistance, and sensitive about their current strategic importance and vulnerability.

The Germans left a physical as well as a psychological imprint. Huge cave bunkers and concrete gun emplacements are scattered around the country. The Norwegians eventually found that it was more trouble than it was worth trying to destroy the bunkers and decided to use them instead. Some of the marines' pre-positioned supplies are kept in them in central Norway, and the marine brigade's headquarters for this exercise is down the road from Evenes at the Tarstad bunker.

Cut into the side of a small hill on the edge of the Ofot Fjord, the bunker has immense steel doors that open into a long tunnel with dank walls that, in turn, lead into deeply recessed chambers. Built by Russian slave laborers, whose bodies were tossed into the fjord after they died from malnourishment and exhaustion, the Tarstad bunker retains an aura of desperation and evil that even the homely atmosphere of the marines' kitchen, with its TV set, familiar sauce bottles, and cautionary notices ("Keep Our Kitchen Clean"), cannot entirely dispel.

There are a few days before the exercise begins, and the marines, in different locations, are preparing for battle. An interesting aspect of this particular operation is the presence of a battalion of reservists, who have unfurled their colors in a Norwegian workers' holiday chalet complex along the fjord. They are from the Second Battalion of the Twenty-fourth Marine Regiment, whose battle honors include Iwo Jima and who are commanded by a Chicago lawyer.

Organized on a territorial basis, the Marine Corps reserves are designed to muster an extra division in time of war. Reservists, who may once have been active-duty

marines but who, even if they haven't, will have graduated from boot camp or Quantico officers school, train two days a month and go to field camp for two weeks a year. The officers and men of 2/24 all come from Illinois and include bankers, teachers, real estate developers, policemen, bakers, the vice-president of a brewery, plumbers, electricians, and kids who work in grocery stores.

"We like to feel we are in the Marine Corps," says the battalion operations officer, who works for a computer firm when he isn't wearing marine green. "None of us likes the 'weekend warrior' tag. Nor do we like the term 'reservist.' We all want to be here, we've trained hard, and most of us can ski. We're just marines on reserve duty."

Marine reserve units used to have a tendency to be cozy old boys' clubs but this, says the commanding officer of 2/24, has changed in recent years. Reservists have to earn their place and their rank, and the whole process is closely monitored by the regimental headquarters and the regular Marine Corps cadre that helps train the reserve units. The reservists claim there is no real difference between their performance in the field and the skills of active-duty marines. The latter tend to shrug and say, well yes, and what they can't do, they make up for in enthusiasm.

Some reservists spend a great deal more time soldiering than their minimum requirement. There is a toll-free number in Kansas City where a marine master sergeant tells reservists what's going on and when and how they can fit in. Some reservists are ready to go at the drop of a hat—like a public affairs captain on this exercise who keeps her uniform handy in her bedroom closet. Others are more inaccessible, such as a colonel who is a specialist in winter warfare and who also happens to be an Alaskan commercial fisherman. The Marine Corps has to contact the Coast Guard to reach him.

For the "floaters," the scenario goes something like this, according to the Washington lawyer (whose line from the film *Casablanca* was so ill received on boarding the Flying Tigers flight): "I phone Kansas City to find out what's going on," he says. "The master sergeant suggests Camp Lejeune, North Carolina, in April and I say, 'Sorry, Top, calendar full.' Then he says: 'How about Norway next week?' And I say, 'You're on.' It's great to climb into uniform, curse, smoke a cigar, and go downtown and create hell in a bar. No one minds. They shrug and say: 'He's a marine.' Do that as a Washington tax lawyer, and you'll be disbarred. And when I come back from the wars," he continues, "I order my staff around like a general would."

Day One of Cold Winter is a bit chaotic. A walk down the road reveals a couple of marine vehicles in a ditch, half buried in deep, soft snow. In one of them sits the regimental commander who had briefed his men in the theater at Fort McCoy. He is studying a map and smoking a cigar while his driver waits for help to arrive. The colonel shrugs philosophically. "Fortunes of war," he says. "The driver now knows a bit more about handling a vehicle in the snow."

Units are so spread out that it is hard to find them. The controllers, however, say that everything is going according to plan. A Dutch Marine company has been wiped out, the British paras are holding their own, and all U.S. Marine units are doing well, although the commanding general narrowly escaped capture by an advancing column of Norwegian Leopard tanks.

On Day Two the action becomes more visible and noisier. U.S. Air Force A-10 Thunderbolts circle and swoop. Nicknamed "warthogs" on account of their undeniable ugliness, the A-10s are providing close air support for the "enemy." Marine helicopters thud and flap their way over the snowy landscape, moving troops, lifting supplies, and every now and again picking up a reconnaissance unit that has done its stuff and is in danger of being overrun. The marines' elegant new superfighters, the F/A 18 Hornets, zoom in low over the fjords, spreading a notional havoc before them.

One of the marines' defensive positions is a place called Tjeldsund, a bleak but beautiful island linked to the mainland by a bridge that looks as if it had been found on the cutting-room floor of *A Bridge Too Far.* (As the winter sun sinks, burnishing the slate-colored waters of the fjord, you can almost see the bucket-helmeted German guards cross in the center of the bridge, exchange a few words, blow on their hands, and pace on.)

Under the cover of some pines down by the water's edge, a cluster of marine amphibious assault vehicles, or AAVs, squats waiting for the order to "swim." Their drivers call them "hogs" or "pigs," but they're immensely proud of this most marine of vehicles. Legend has it that the notion of an amphibious troop-carrying vehicle came from the time when a truck accidentally fell off a ship and floated. True or not, the amphibious tractor, or amtrac, as it used to be called, enabled the marines to carve out their unique beach-storming role in the Pacific campaigns of World War II. "When you talk Marine Corps, you're talking this vehicle," says the lieutenant commanding the unit.

On Day Three the enemy, according to the scenario, is closing in. Halfway up a hill on Tjelsund, a platoon is digging in for a rest after moving for most of the night. The weather has been kind: no fresh snow, little wind, and a night temperature of only 10 degrees below freezing. The marines cut out snow bricks with their machetes and construct makeshift bivouacs. In addition to rifle and ammunition, they carry a sleeping bag, an insulation pad to put under it, extra supplies of socks for sweaty feet produced by the thermal boots, and solid fuel for cooking three days' worth of dehydrated food.

Meals Ready to Eat, or MREs, have replaced the old C-rations. These are the latest brainchild of the military planners, and although they weigh less than "C-rats" they are virtually inedible without water. The marines wrap the sealed packages around their bodies to keep such delights as ham and chicken loaf ("dead man in a pack") warm and malleable. The British rations have more variety as well as such exotica as curry and rice. The marines, in an attempt to make the MREs more interesting, sometimes mash everything together and garnish the unsightly result with hot Louisiana sauce. By the last day of the exercise, MRE has a new definition: "Meals Rejected by Ethiopians."

Day Four shows signs of fatigue: a jeep driver is asleep at the wheel near a battalion command post; a column of amphibious assault vehicles, whose camouflage is a bit sloppy, are all pointing in the same direction and apparently unguarded; a marine is walking along a road with a couple of Norwegian girls, no doubt on an intelligence mission; piles of garbage in the snow indicate a distinctly American presence. "You the writer?" asks a disgruntled driver. "Write this shit sucks!"

But the war isn't over yet. A reconnaissance unit that has spent five days behind enemy lines in a burned-out house emerges from the fjord, dragging its Zodiac rubber boat up the beach. "We had to get out fast last night," says one of them, looking strangely scruffy and bearded for a marine. "The Royal Marines dropped some guys by helicopter and it was time to go." "Recon" people, the sharp end of the Marine Corps, carry seventy-pound packs and spend a lot of time in small boats, parachuting, scuba diving, and following other manly pursuits. But they wear nicer gear, especially the brown Buffalo jackets, and eat better food, notably the LURP or long-range patrol rations. "You'd kill for LURP food," says another recon man.

What happens if you get caught? The standard instructions, says an officer back at headquarters, are: "If you're captured, remember: name, rank, and serial number — and eat the map."

On Day Five it's time to look at the air wing based at Bodo airfield well south of where the action is taking place. One of the truly unique aspects of the United States Marine Corps is the close, indeed, intimate embrace between its ground and air forces. All marine officers, whether they are platoon commanders, fighter pilots, communications wizards, "beans, bullets, and bandages" logisticians, public affairs impresarios, tankers, artillerymen — whoever puts on the gold bars of a second lieutenant — go through the same officer training at Quantico. No other service does that.

Equally important, marine air power is totally at the service of marine ground

Following pages
Infantry in an unusual setting for marines — Exercise Cold Winter: Arctic Circle, Norway
Light Armored Vehicles (LAV) on patrol in Norway. An eight-wheeled lightly armored vehicle, the LAV mounts a 25mm automatic cannon and can travel up to ninety miles an hour
Reconnaissance unit beaches its Zodiac on the icy shore of a Norwegian fjord

power, forging a formidable weapon on the battlefield. "What this means," says the commanding general, looking tactical with a .45 strapped across his chest, "is a powerful synergistic effect between the air and ground elements, much faster and more effective than, say, between the army and the air force."

In practice it means a platoon commander, even a squad leader, can call in air support from a range of lethal and very fast-flying machines to deliver death and destruction to the enemy in front of him . . . and all at the drop of a hat, assuming the aircraft are within flying range, radios function, and the man on the ground can read a map.

Throughout the exercise the F/A 18 Hornets, which replaced the F-4 Phantoms, so long the fighter-bomber workhorse of the Marine Corps, have been flying sortie after sortie. The pilots tend to be small, rather unassuming men with a confident bounce in their stride, as well they might, careening through the sky in their $28-million state-of-the-art fighters.

Old Phantom pilots call the Hornet the "electric jet" on account of its high degree of computerization. The new pilots come from the "Pac-man" generation; computers and fingertip controls are as familiar to them as stick shifts were to their predecessors. "If you've grown up killing a lot of aliens in a video arcade, it helps flying this bird," says a major who converted from Phantoms.

The Hornet squadron flew over from its home base in Beaufort, South Carolina. Refueling in the air every forty-five to sixty minutes, the 3,700-mile journey to Edinburgh in Scotland took eight hours, most of it at night. The computerized inertial navigation system guided the squadron to within half a mile of its destination. Some of the pilots brought hamburgers and fried chicken with them, heating up the food on the defroster; coats and ties for "liberty" were stashed behind the pilot's seat. And what about . . . ? "Number one is taken care of by a rubber bladder in the cockpit," says a pilot. "Number two? You hold on to it."

At the end of the exercise in Bodo, the air wing takes stock. The most impressive bit of high-tech wizardry is the FLIR, or Forward Looking Infra-Red device, a kind of video camera that is mounted in the nose of the Hornet. Operated at night, the FLIR produces an astonishingly clear videotape of anything it is aimed at. The marines flew over the invading British fleet during the first night of the exercise, and the pilots now watch the results on a standard television screen. Flying at nine thousand feet, at 2:30 A.M., the British fleet is seen moving slowly up the fjord as if it were being filmed in broad daylight. As the flotilla unfolds, the pilot gives a running commentary: "Helo pad on back of landing ship . . . helo on deck with its blades folded . . . eight large ships to the north, five to the south."

There are occasional video game beeps indicating a radar warning of anti-aircraft missiles. When he is not talking, you can hear the pilot breathing into his oxygen mask, a rasping sound reminiscent of Darth Vader taking a nap. The "show" ends with scenes of the British troops landing. The images are so clear that individuals can be seen working on the decks of the ships. "We could have wiped out the lot of them on Day One," says the air-wing commander.

Back in Evenes, it is post-mortem time. "The weather was bad," says a Norwegian controller, "because it wasn't bad enough." A marine lieutenant leads his platoon down a snowy slope, heading back to base. He is freshly shaved. "That was the toughest week in their lives," he says nodding to his weary men. Lack of sleep, sweaty clothes—it's hot when you move and freezing when you don't—and lack of hot food were the worst problems.

"When we first started coming to Norway," says an officer who was there in the early days, "everyone used to laugh at our Korean War-vintage winter gear. They used to call us the Michelin men, our stuff was so heavy and cumbersome, and we couldn't ski worth a damn. They gave us high marks for intestinal fortitude and low marks for military activity."

In the nature of Allied war games, no one really won and no one really lost Exercise Cold Winter. But the marine grunts had made their point. They had proved they could hack it in the arctic even though the food wasn't great, the helos didn't always land in the right place, and, from time to time, the whole thing sucked. But, according to marine lore, a bitching marine is a good marine, and that doesn't change—whatever the temperature is.

The Philippines

U.S.S. PELELIU

The ship is steaming along the coast of the Philippines, a dozen miles or so off the U.S. naval base at Subic Bay, under a brilliant sun and through calm seas. Named after the Pacific island assaulted and captured by the First Marine Division in October 1944, the *Peleliu* is one of the fleet's newest landing helicopter assault ships (LHAs). Fifth in its class, it displaces thirty-nine thousand tons, is 820 feet long, travels at more than twenty knots, is armed with two five-inch and six 20mm guns and two close-in weapons systems, and carries a crew of 880 officers and enlisted men. Its purpose in life is to project marine power onto a hostile shore in the time-honored fashion.

"U.S.S. *Peleliu*," says the navy handout, "was designed to maintain what the Marine Corps call 'tactical integrity'—getting a balanced force to the same point at the same time. *Peleliu* can carry a complete Marine Battalion Landing Team [BLT], along with the supplies and equipment needed in an assault, and land them ashore by helicopter and/or amphibious craft. This two-pronged capability, with emphasis on vertical launch and landing troops and equipment, aids the Navy-Marine Corps team in carrying out its present-day mission."

The *Peleliu* can carry almost two thousand marines, up to thirty-five helicopters, and six Harrier "jump" jets on deck and a large number of amphibious vehicles, tanks, guns, trucks, ammunition, and supplies in its capacious belly. It looks like a new breed of stocky aircraft carrier, which is what it is, although its venom lies in its innards rather than on its decks or in its superstructure.

The *Peleliu* has a secondary, humanitarian function: it doubles as an evacuation disaster relief and hospital ship. It can carry hundreds of tons of medical supplies and food, provide electric power and fresh water from its engineering plant, and move up to two thousand evacuees. Below decks there is a modern three-hundred-bed hospital and facilities to treat several hundred outpatients.

There are now about a thousand marines on board engaged in a variety of exercises. On the flight deck, several helicopters whine and shudder as they prepare to take off. They are taking troops ashore for an exercise that simulates the evacuation of American citizens from a fictional U.S. consular office in the island nation of "Purple." The Americans are endangered, the scenario goes, because of threats made by the "Purple Liberation Front" and the inability of the "Purple" government to guarantee their security.

A CH-53, the marines' largest helicopter transport, sits immobilized in a corner, its wings folded back, looking like a giant, malevolent moth. Below, in the cavernous well deck, the navy's new amphibious toy, a military version of the hovercraft, known prosaically—and ass backward—as the Landing Craft Air Cushion or LCAC, is getting ready to launch.

Designed to carry such heavy equipment as trucks and tanks, the LCAC can skim over land and water alike at speeds of up to fifty knots. This one is loaded with the marines' new equivalent of the jeep—a larger and more versatile vehicle with another ponderous acronym that boils down to "Hum-Vee"—and nine reconnaissance marines

Jungle patrol:
Subic Bay, Philippines
Following pages
Amtracs launched
for a beach assault in
the Pacific
Flight-deck operations
on the U.S.S. *Peleliu*

accompanied by their rubber boats, radios, weapons, and rations. Square, squat, and gray, with two huge fans mounted on the rear, the LCAC begins to puff itself up like a monstrous toad. There is a high-pitched roar of turbines and the smell of aviation fuel. The sea bubbles and boils at the mouth of the well deck as the mother ship steams sedately along.

A sailor wearing a red helmet and waving two illuminated batons signals all clear. The sea turns into a fury of spume as the craft that is neither boat nor plane but something in between lifts up off the deck, air puffing up indecorously around its skirt, and backs out into the ocean. It turns slowly and then speeds off toward the horizon, leaving behind it a curtain of moisture, the smell of gasoline, and a small sense of wonderment.

JUNGLE PATROL

Down in A Company headquarters, Marine Barracks, in Subic Bay, marines are preparing for a jungle patrol. There are three pictures in the company commander's office: Belleau Wood; Iwo Jima; and Lieutenant General Lewis "Chesty" Puller. The company commander, a young captain, has a Virginia country accent that he either cannot or does not want to lose.

"Our job is to provide patrols twenty-four hours a day in the jungle on the base's northern perimeter," he says. "It's a big area, one hundred fifty thousand acres or so, and there are three marine companies involved. There is a training side to it, but the main purpose is to strengthen the security of the base."

The principal threat, apparently, is not from communist insurgents but what the military tactfully terms "economic intruders"—that is, poachers, thieves, and other socially undesirable elements. The American base and its housing represent a powerful magnet to the Filipino criminal, who is both a resourceful individual and at home in the jungle. Thieves have been known to trek through the jungle, break into a house on the base, and walk back through the rain forest with refrigerators, air conditioners, and television sets on their backs. Their taste is eclectic; a favorite item is the all-American plastic trash can, which is sold for the equivalent of twenty-five dollars.

A patrol, which has already donned its camouflage greasepaint, is in the briefing room listening to a sergeant going over the details of the terrain to be covered that night. The patrol will leave at 10:00 P.M., walk into position, and set up ambushes during the night. It will be picked up by truck at a prearranged spot at 6:00 A.M. In addition to the marines in the patrol, there is a Filipino guard who is an employee of the U.S. Defense Department and who acts as interpreter. If there any arrests to be made, he will make them.

The marines carry their standard M-16A2 rifle with sixty rounds of ammunition each, but one member of the patrol has a twelve-gauge shotgun instead. They also take Ka-Bars, the marines' issue fighting knife, a radio, flashlights, two canteens of water each, and dry rations. The Filipino guard is armed with a .38 revolver.

The opposition will be equipped with a quixotic but potentially deadly arsenal of weapons that includes knives, *bolos* (a local machete), blow guns, and even bows and arrows. The sergeant goes through the checklist on the rules of engagement and the use of deadly force. Marines, who patrol with live rounds in their magazines, may fire in self-defense or if a comrade is attacked, and sometimes they do just that. The sergeant recounts an incident where an "economic intruder" attacked a marine with a *bolo* and was shot in the legs for his pains.

There are other enemies, common to all jungles. The snakes are mainly cobras, pythons, and the bamboo viper. There are also wild boars, which are dangerous if sows with piglets are encountered. Wild carabaos (water buffaloes), monkeys, soldier ants, monitor lizards, leeches, and the omnipresent mosquito complete the animal kingdom.

But there are also friendly forces in the jungle, namely the Negritos, small, wiry, African-looking forest dwellers who are the original inhabitants of the Philippines.

They are largely nomadic and make a precarious living from hunting, fishing, wood-carving, as well as more modern pursuits such as finding and selling golf balls. They are excellent trackers and often help the marines locate intruders.

A point man is selected, ambush teams assigned, and radio frequencies checked. The sergeant goes to the map. "It's a six-click [kilometer] hump," he says. "Let's go."

A thin, scrawny corporal, who chews tobacco and has a country accent, leads his squad up a steep trail with a red laterite floor and a dark green canopy overhead. "I seen a lot of stuff," he says. "We collared sixty-seven intruders in mah time. Got hit in the face once and another time an old woman took a lunge at me with a knife. Never boring," he grunts, squirting tobacco juice at a column of red ants as big as grasshoppers.

A group of Negritos with their pye dogs passes by. Negrito children are laughing and splashing in the river down below. The patrol had noticed some freshly cut bamboo earlier and staked out the area for three hours, but nothing happened. An abandoned *nipa* (bamboo) hut by the river had received the same attention with the same result. Old marines who patrolled other jungles in other times will recognize the pattern. "That's where the base gets its drinking water from," says the corporal with a grin, pointing his rifle at the muddy stream.

The sergeant, wiping the sweat off his forehead, says the marines like it in the Philippines because it is the only place where they do real live jungle patrols twenty-four hours a day, three hundred and sixty-five days a year, with live rounds. The corporal grins again. "Yeah, they also like the liberty," he says, "Olongapo, Subic, Angeles City—nothing wrong with that."

What about the climate?

"Beats freezin'," replies the sergeant laconically as he moves up the trail.

29 Palms, California

The Marine Corps is the owner of vast tracts of land of feudal proportions, none of which is more valuable, in military if not traditional real estate terms, than the 930 square miles of the Mojave Desert in California known as 29 Palms.

This expanse of rock, sand, and mountain, about an hour's drive due east of Palm Springs and twenty-six hundred feet above sea level, doubles as desert-training and live-fire terrain for combined units of marines. It is here that infantry, tanks, light-armored vehicles, guns, fighter aircraft, helicopter gunships, reconnaissance units, demolition experts, communicators, combat engineers, and all the logistics people play for as real as they can, short of facing an authentic enemy that actually shoots back. It is all summed up by the acronym CAX, combined arms exercises.

The scenario for these war games, which run throughout the year, remains constant. There is a notional amphibious landing the day before the exercise begins. The "enemy" is the "Mojavians," who use Soviet equipment and tactics. The assault through the desert has a number of scripted tactical reverses to test the ingenuity of commanders, and the whole thing lasts two and a half days. Moonless nights are always chosen. Temperatures in the summer range from over 120 degrees Fahrenheit during the day to the forties at night. Scorpions, tarantulas, rattlesnakes, centipedes, sand fleas, and mosquitoes allow for unscripted personal reverses.

The most dramatic difference between this and other exercises is that everyone who has a gun barrel, an artillery tube, rocket pod, or anything else that spits out lethal ordnance uses it. From the grunt in his sandy foxhole, clutching his M-16A2 rifle, to the 155mm self-propelled howitzers and the Harrier vertical takeoff fighters carrying bombs and rockets, every breech is loaded with the right stuff. The result is a lot of noise ("rock-and-roll city," says the public affairs man), some danger, and a better sense of what combat might be like. The exercise is primarily designed for battalion-sized units and is a test of a commander's ability to coordinate all the different sources of firepower at his disposal—from the air, ground, and sea—and to improvise if one element or another fails to do the job.

It is 7:00 A.M. on the line of departure on a small rocky hilltop in the Mojave Desert. The air is cold, crisp, and brittle. It is easier to understand why rocks crack during the night in desert climates. It is too cold for scorpions but not cold enough to stiffen the ink in a pen, and beyond the blue shadows of the mountains the eastern horizon is beginning to lighten. The desert floor is spread out below, a broad, gently curving valley that extends for several miles before tapering off into a narrow pass between jagged cliffs. It is along this valley that the assault will take place.

The bombardment starts with the heavy crash of eight-inch howitzers hurling their shells up to fourteen miles. Their role is to simulate the naval gunfire that would support a marine amphibious assault. The marines' artillery joins in. Puffs of smoke and dust rise in the distance as the shells rain down, followed by the echoing crump of the explosions. Twin-hulled OV-10 reconnaissance planes wheel overhead like seagulls, beady eyes on their prey. Two Cobra gunships suddenly appear in a cleft in the hills, well below the summit, and hover menacingly. A pair of FA/18 Hornet fighters scream low over the crest, roll to their left, and are gone.

And then comes a sound that never fails to thrill or chill: the metallic groaning and squeaking of a column of armor on the move. There is something especially awesome about the sight of tanks moving across a desert, evoking the great tank battles in North Africa during World War II and the clash of armor between the Egyptians and Israelis in the Sinai Desert in the 1973 Arab-Israeli War. Firing as they grind along, the tanks' 105mm cannon make a sharper and more distinctive crack than the longer "vroomph" of the artillery. On each flank of the column there is a TOW (wire-guided antitank missile) carried on the back of a light truck; they act as the column's "side eyes," watching out for hostile armor. The two Cobra gunships, still hovering in a fold of the hills, also have a protective role, since modern technology has rendered the once almighty tank much more vulnerable to attack and destruction than in the past.

Amphibious assault vehicles (AAVs), which are tracked and lightly armored, have appeared and are belching out black smoke as they crunch over the stony plain. They look strangely out of place in this waterless wilderness—at a distance their profile resembles the Dutch peasant's wooden sabot or shoe—but the camouflage on all the vehicles blends in well with the desert's gray rock, tawny sand, and green shrubs. A group of AAVs moves across in front, their M-60 machine guns spewing red tracer bullets into the hillside.

There is the stuttering thud of .50-caliber machine guns mounted on top of the tanks, opening up on targets in a ravine. The infantry moves up in five-ton trucks and then deploys on foot, one rifle company on the left flank and the other on the right. A visiting marine general turns to an aide. "Is the infantry outflanking the mine field?" he asks. "I don't think they've figured out what to do yet, sir," the aide replies, peering through his binoculars.

A spotter plane comes over and drops white phosphorus flares on the "mine field" as a marker for the Harrier fighters that sweep in and drop their one-thousand-pound bombs. After a decent pause, the infantry gets on the move again. In another sector, however, the exercise controllers, who race around in vehicles flying white flags, consider that a group of tanks and AAVs walked into a trap, having failed to identify the strength of the enemy properly and neutralize it before advancing. The tanks turn their turrets around, guns pointing back the way they came, to show that they are "dead."

There is a lull, and we move forward to the front line. Some tanks have tucked themselves into shallow depressions in the sand and become virtually invisible. A red flag marks a partially exploded bomb from a Harrier; it is "safe," according to an ordnance man who has driven up in a jeep with the side doors fastened open in case he and his engineers have to bail out in a hurry.

There is a sudden whoosh from behind us, very close. Everyone instinctively ducks or hits the sand. A line charge of high explosives has been fired from an AAV at a forward "mine field." But the rocket propelling it separated and shot off into the blue yonder, leaving the charge draped over the AAV. The ordnance man races off. He returns to say everything is cool. The charge, which contains seventeen hundred pounds of high explosive, remains inert unless it is fully extended and electronically detonated by hand. "Strange, though," he adds reflectively. "That's only the second time it has happened in the past ten years."

The "battle" continues as the sun reaches its zenith and begins its slow descent. The troops have moved several miles forward along the valley. The place names on the map illustrate the recent history of this barren land: Bullion Mountains, Miners' Pass, and Gypsum Ridge. Toward evening, the tempo slows and the men eat their chow in their foxholes. Over to one side of the valley the head controller, a lieutenant colonel from Tennessee, is setting up a portable barbecue grill. He pulls out a small bag of charcoal, lights up, and lays a thick steak on top of the grill.

He is Coyote Five, the master orchestrator of the live-fire exercises, and he spends a good part of his time out in the desert. "The old call sign for controllers was 'Snow White,'" he says with a grin. "But we changed it to 'Coyote' because we stink."

A lost 81mm mortar crew drives up in a truck to find out where their mortars are. The lieutenant colonel takes out a well-worn map and shows them where the unit should be. "This is the only part of the Marine Corps in peacetime that thinks tactical every day," he says. "It's also the closest that a young marine will get to combat, short of the real thing. Here he'll be within a thousand yards of artillery and air-to-ground fire.

"We try to make it as realistic as possible in that we start with full tanks of fuel, new batteries, good tires, and so on. But we will tell units that they are experiencing real-life problems such as a broken axle, the radio's knocked out, it's time to refuel, there are casualties to be evacuated, and so on. Of course, a lot of things you don't have to set up. We started with seventeen tanks today and four have already broken down. We also throw down CS gas every now and then so the troops have to put on their gas masks pretty damn fast."

He prods the steak with a fork. "The key thing about all this is the close air support. No other service has that kind of support, but we need it because we are thin skinned on the ground." What about the navy? In a war, it seems likely that navy air power would be called on to support the marines on the ground at some stage. Do they "play" with the marines here? "Occasionally," says the lieutenant colonel. "They've been here with their FA/18 fighters three or four times in the last twenty-seven exercises. They were particularly good last time. Very pumped up."

What about desert fighting? "Water, obviously, is the critical thing," he says. "The old idea was that you had water discipline—that is, you rationed yourself very carefully. We believe you should drink as much as you can. In fact, you must push yourself to drink because you don't notice sweat in a desert climate. In the summer, when the thermometer is up around 130 degrees, you need three to five gallons a day to fight and survive in this environment."

It is time for the real "rock-and-roll city," the night firing. We stand on a hill about three hundred feet above the valley floor, which is crisscrossed with countless tank and tire tracks. The marines are strung out from mountain wall to mountain wall. They squat in shallow foxholes, partially covered with their sleeping bags against the growing, bone-aching cold. The amphibious assault vehicles are already dug in with camouflage nets over them. Giant scoops in the sand have been prepared for the tanks to hunker down for the night.

There is a long wait as the light slowly bleeds out of the biblical landscape. A master sergeant, who is stamping his feet and blowing on his hands, blames the delay on the top brass. "They're just starting their cocktails," he says. He and a couple of other staff NCOs bemoan the demise of hard drinking and carousing in the corps. "I hear it's no longer 'Happy Hour' in the Officers' Club," he says, "but 'Social Time.' It used to be 'Animal Hour' in the Enlisted Men's Club in my day."

They also talk about some of the crazy things that happen out in the desert. "There was a recon guy here once," says a gunny. "He tried to bite the head off a rattlesnake and had to be evacuated with a tongue the size of a football. Some of the marines get bored and play with tarantulas. And then there was that tank crew who lost their bearings and shot up the hill where the commanding general and all his staff were standing."

Old marines talk about the corps the way most people talk about family. One minute the subject is the new commandant who was here not so long ago and turned down some of the perks that go with the job. "He asked for a marine blanket, GI toilet paper, and C-rations," says another staff NCO approvingly. "How about that!"

The next minute, it's the new German-style Kevlar helmet, which, they all complain, ain't good for nothin'. You can't wash in it, you can't cook in it, and you can't dig with it. They talk about the few nightspots in the area and about the big Swedish broad who manages one of them and can physically toss out any marine who gets juiced up; about places they've been to—Vietnam, Korea, Japan, the Philippines. "Them Filipino girls are *used* to a lotta cock," says the master sergeant laconically.

The shoot begins after a three-hour wait in the cold. The mountains have all but vanished in the gloom; there is a canopy of stars but no moon. Spotter planes drop white and gold flares far down the valley and the artillery opens up with a roar. Harriers and Cobras, wheeling in different layers of starlit sky, tilt and attack. Flares move down the valley toward us. Red tracer, being fired horizontally, shows that tanks are in action. A spotter plane hits one of the illuminated "enemy" targets with a rocket and a ragged cheer comes up from the valley below. Then, out of the darkness, comes the sound of tanks. The whine of engines, the squeak of cogs and wheels, and the clank of metal treads on a resisting surface grow louder. Three hundred feet above it is a primitive, exciting sound, the sound of a Leviathan whose power has been unleashed on an unsuspecting world. Slowly, the whole column can be seen, moving fast, throwing up great clouds of dust and exhaust. The ground shakes and the chill down your spine has nothing to do with the cold.

The Harrier airfield is strictly tactical and very temporary. It is situated at a place called Surprise Springs, some seven miles from the main base, and it is designed to support the battalion-sized live-fire exercise that is going on the other side of the mountains. It is the first time that an improvised airstrip has been laid down in the desert at 29 Palms, according to the young-looking lieutenant colonel who is in charge of it all. (He is also a former F-4 Phantom pilot who has converted to the FA/18 Hornet.) The strip was built of aluminum matting by marine engineers in two days. There are two hundred men in the detachment, including fourteen pilots for the seven Harriers. "Everything's pretty realistic," says the lieutenant colonel, "except the three-hole shitter." He points to a row of plastic portable toilets. "The environmentalists like us to keep the desert clean."

The idea is to create the sort of hostile, makeshift conditions that the versatile Harrier "jump jet" might have to work from in a shooting war. Every attempt is made to simulate combat conditions during the two-and-a-half day exercise. "We use nothing but live ordnance," says the lieutenant colonel. "If you don't have the right ordnance and you get a call for close air support from the infantry, you've got to find another way to skin the cat. It's a dangerous business, too. There's great potential for hurting people."

In the cold ashen light of a desert dawn, we drive out to Surprise Springs, passing a prospector's ruined house, three windblown palm trees, and a couple of coyotes on the prowl. In the distance Bear Mountain has some early winter snow on its peak. Colors are being called at the airstrip. A whistle is blown, everyone stops in his tracks and salutes, the flag is raised, and it is all over. "We don't believe in much of a show here," says a major, buttoning up his leather flight jacket. "The show's on the runway."

Seven Harriers, muscular-looking fighters with short, almost stubby swept-back wings, sit there ready for action. Developed from the British AV8As ("a sports car of a plane," says one pilot), the Harrier has been with the Marine Corps since the early seventies and is the only vertical and short takeoff attack aircraft in the United States armed forces. The new model, the AV8B, is larger, faster, and handles better than its predecessor, a Cadillac by comparison. "It will do anything in the air," says another enthusiastic pilot. "It can take off and land vertically, hover, turn, go backward, bow to the crowd, even sign autographs."

They can also land virtually anywhere—on roads, aircraft-carrier decks, aluminum matting strips like the one here, on grass clearings in the jungle, and even in parking lots. The British, who used them with great success in the Falklands War in 1982, once put a Harrier down on a container ship. "They're very forgiving aircraft," says a veteran pilot.

All marine air power is designed to provide close support for the infantry ever since marine pilots pioneered the concept in Nicaragua in the late twenties. But the Harrier is the marines' fighter, *par excellence.* Painted marine green, the Harriers shadow the infantry, flying low and fast off assault ships or tactical airstrips just a few minutes in the air from the people they are designed to protect. "Our thing is amphibious assault, softening up the beach, and close air support for the grunt on the ground," says the major.

The planes have their critics though. The vertical takeoff is not of great tactical value because the aircraft can carry very little ordnance under those circumstances. It is not as fast or as electronically sophisticated as the FA/18 Hornet, nor as deadly as the snout-nosed A-6 Intruder, which humps a much heavier load of weaponry. Some critics believe it was a mistake to replace the 30mm tank-killing cannon on the earlier version of the Harrier with the lighter 25mm Gatling gun, which lacks sufficient punch to destroy tanks.

And every now and again, a Harrier will drop out of the sky when something goes wrong during those palm-sweating moments of vertical descent. (One did just that at 29 Palms three months earlier when a fuel line got blocked as it came in to land. Fortunately, the pilot managed to eject safely.) But none of this makes much of an impression on a Harrier pilot, even those who originally wanted to fly Hornets and didn't make it. "They're super birds," is the inevitable response.

A pair of Harriers, their engines warming, are on a fifteen-minute alert. It will take them six minutes from where they are on the runway to the target area fourteen miles away. Two more are being loaded up with one-thousand-pound bombs, Zuni rockets, and antipersonnel cluster bombs known as Rockeye, a sort of modern grapeshot that can turn an area as large as a football field into a killing ground. The two forward Harriers have received the word to go. The armorers run forward to arm the rockets, and the pilots raise their hands in the cockpit to show they are not touching the controls. With a shattering roar, they take off into the gray sky, circle quickly, and disappear over the mountain ridge. Up above, two more Harriers are being refueled in the air, like twins on their mother's breasts. The airstrip is two thousand feet long, but a fully loaded Harrier needs only about six hundred feet to become airborne. A Hornet, carrying the same load, requires five times that distance.

Some of the pilots are talking about the previous night's exercise. "Night flying is like night marching," says one. "It's scary. Being up is good, but landing is the problem. At night there's no color, so your depth perception goes. If you hear someone say he likes flying at night—beware. It's like saying the check's in the mail, one of the ten big lies."

Under exercise rules, ordnance cannot be dropped closer to the infantry than one thousand yards. In a real war, however, the Harrier pilots would be unloading their stuff

Harrier pilots
Harriers
Following pages
Helo rush hour
in the midday heat:
29 Palms
Helicopters flying
in for the assault during
a CAX at 29 Palms
AH-1 Cobra gunship
firing a Zuni rocket
at a target in the desert
"Rock-and-roll city":
night firing in the
Mojave Desert

as close as three hundred yards. "The fragmentation range of a five-hundred-pound bomb," says another pilot, "is roughly the length of this airfield, which means that our troops would get some of the pieces. But that's what you need when the other guys are coming through the wire."

Like the Harriers, the Cobra helicopter gunships are close-in aerial fighters. "We can fly under and over the arcs of artillery fire," says a Cobra pilot. "Big sky, little bullet," the saying goes. Cobras, aptly named, are lean, mean, humped-back machines with a two-man crew. The pilot sits behind the gunner in a raised seat, but he can fire everything except the antitank TOW missile from his rear position. The gunships are formidably armed. A Cobra can carry cannon, rockets, heat-seeking missiles such as the laser-guided Hellfire or the wire-guided TOW, antipersonnel cluster bombs, and "chaff" and other decoy devices. Developed from the small "Huey" transport helicopter, the Cobra gunships came into their own in Vietnam and have remained an important part of the Marine Corps' inventory ever since. Their pilots, who think they have the best job in the Marine Corps, favor such macho call signs as Gunfighter, Tiger, Evil Eye, and Nightmare.

Aloft in a Huey, we follow a pair of Cobras going into the attack. The gunships fly low over the plain, hugging the lee of ridges, following the contours and occasionally vanishing from view as they blend with the dun-colored hills. Their feel for cover in the air is rather like that of an experienced infantryman's sense of terrain on the ground. The Cobras bank and fly through a cleft in the hills, take a quick look around a ridge, back off, and hover like two watchful dragonflies. A column of vehicles, evenly spaced and throwing up clouds of dust, churns along a track in the next valley. We settle down on a hilltop, bobbing up and down in our seats as the rotor continues to spin and the engine whines. There's something wrong with the radio. The crew chief takes a tin of chewing tobacco from his flight jacket and puts a plug in the corner of his mouth.

Artillery rounds burst down below. We take off again and follow the Cobras. From the air, the eroded ridges look like dried leaves with atrophied veins. The myriad tracks of vehicles resemble hieroglyphics, and the shrubs scattered over the valley produce the effect of unshaven stubble. The Cobras disappear into a narrow ravine. We fly over the top of the ridge and see them hovering over the target, one at a slightly higher elevation covering the other. The forward gunship fires its Zuni rockets accompanied by a roar and a flash of pale green flame. The barrel of its Gatling gun appears— the snake's tongue—and revolves as it spits bullets out at the rate of 750 rounds a minute. The empty casings dribble out of the breech in a steady flow over the vast graveyard of wrecked vehicles, bomb fragments, rockets and shells, and unexploded ordnance below.

Camp Lejeune, North Carolina

The Marine Corps is geographically positioned to operate across two oceans. It handles the Pacific largely from Camp Pendleton in southern California, where the First Marine Division is based. The Atlantic is addressed from Camp Lejeune, in Jacksonville, North Carolina, where the Second Marine Division has its home. These two vast bases ("camp" is a serious misnomer) also accommodate many ancillary units, schools, and specialized facilities. Around them is a growing population of families, civilian workers and suppliers, and retired marines. The Marine Corps may seem small in comparison with the other armed services, but when you are lost and driving around Pendleton or Lejeune, it appears infinite. Camp Lejeune has sixty-one thousand acres, nine miles of beach, and more than forty thousand marines. "Lejeune is a city," says the general in charge.

Camps Lejeune and Pendleton are where the newly minted marine from boot camp comes to learn what it is like to be an infantryman. The infantry course lasts eight weeks, and in the old days all marines, whatever their specialty, did it. Then the practice lapsed. The new commandant, who wants to make every marine a rifleman again, whether pen pusher, wrench handler, or computer key puncher by trade, has reintroduced some basic infantry training for everyone. The schools of infantry in the two bases teach infantry tactics, weapon training, and field exercises, a package of skills that prepares marines for service in the Fleet Marine Forces.

Warm fall sunshine is slanting through the pines, casting flickering shadows on the young marines as they learn their trade. A squad is providing covering fire for a group that is moving cautiously along the treeline toward its objective. Simulated machine gun and rifle fire adds some realism to the exercise. Two men are firing blanks from the Shoulder Launched Multi-purpose Assault Weapon (SMAW for short, bazooka for comprehension). "It is accurate to 250 meters and provides marine infantrymen with the capability to remove urban masonry structures and earth or timber bunkers," says the handout. "The dual-mode warhead discriminates between 'hard' and 'soft' targets."

The assault squads have reached the enemy lines and are learning how difficult and dangerous it can be clearing out a network of trenches and bunkers. A gunnery sergeant in camouflage greasepaint jumps out of a bunker, grabs the rifle barrel of a marine who is creeping along the trench, and gives him a good solid slap on the neck. "That's a knife thrust," he growls.

"Enemy bunker, fifteen meters to the left, is not secure," another marine says to the man behind. "Move out!"

"Don't look down!" yells the gunny, as a marine in the trench drops his gaze from what is happening to pull the pin out of a grenade.

The "enemy," identified by their utility hats turned backward, jump out of a trench farther along the line and fire blanks at the advancing marines. There are a lot of firecracker sounds and yellow smoke. A marine tosses a grenade around a corner into a bunker. A booted foot appears and kicks it back.

"You there," shouts an NCO instructor in faded, starched utilities, "you've got to cover his butt."

"The weapon's jammed, sir."

"I don't care. Get someone else's."

A marine jumps out of a trench awful quick. "Snake!" he screams. An NCO vaults in and kills the small black reptile with a stick.

"We try to make them move with their minds as well as their feet," says the gunny, "but it's difficult getting them to work as a team."

Back in the trenches, the marines are working their way along, flushing the "enemy" out as they move. "Bang, bang, you're dead. Long live Khomeini!" shouts one of the opposing forces who has sneaked up from behind a tree and fired down into the trench. There is a ripple of laughter. "I already shot his ass," says someone else. Boys playing at war. It is hard to sustain realism for long when the bangs are not accompanied by projectiles and the projectiles are not accompanied by broken limbs and mangled guts.

"We used to get the thugs back in the seventies," a staff sergeant says. "You could tell them to do anything, and they'd do it. These kids are more intelligent and ask questions." Would he lead them into combat? "Yes, because I trained them," he replies. "They're all volunteers, and 90 percent of them are highly motivated. We don't have the 'over the wall' problem—absent without leave—that we used to. I'd take 'em."

Another part of the training goes on in Combat Town, a mock-up of an urban environment in which marines might have to fight one day. It's not exactly Hue City, but it has a few of the hazards and obstacles common to any built-up place. A squad, wearing soft hats and carrying rifles, ammunition, and water bottles, zigzags across open ground and clambers onto a roof of a low building by using their rifle slings to pull each other up. They roll over and over along the roof, climb through a window, and then "clear" the rooms inside, one by one. The way out is not the front door but through a second-story window. The marines inch out of the window, turn, hang from the ledge, and drop to the ground. Evasive maneuvering continues across a street and up into the top floor of a three-story building by means of a rope, which has a few helpful knots in it, and some wooden struts on the outside walls to help the climber "walk" up.

"The longer you stay on that wall, the quicker you're goin' to die," shouts an instructor to a slow mover. "Bang, you're dead, the Gooks got you."

Accidents always happen during training. In 1985 thirteen marines drowned off the coast when their helicopter went down. That led to "helicopter egress training," which sounds a bit like the cure that is worse than the disease. Marines, dressed in utilities, are strapped into the body of a helicopter that has several exits but no windows. Once submerged the body is flipped over and the men inside have to get out any way they can. The second time they have to use the front door. They then do the same thing over again, but this time they are blindfolded. An accident of another kind happened while we were at Camp Lejeune. One marine was killed and three others injured when a climbing net collapsed—a supporting spar broke—on an assault course. The moral of the story seems to be that Marine Corps training, while softer and more controlled than it used to be, still has its hazards.

Out at a "tactical landing zone" in the pine woods, four troop-carrying helicopters come in to land. There is the crump of real artillery fire somewhere and the chatter of simulated machine guns. There is a strong smell of cordite. A fine gray dust swirls into the air as the dark green monsters descend. Young marines, wearing combat gear and lugging heavy platoon weapons, jump out. They form a defensive perimeter and stagger off to the treeline, their equipment jingling like a horse's harness. Rough shouts from the NCOs harry the men. "Get on line, move! Let's go, we ain't got all stinkin' day. Get your shit up there." The euphemisms of boot camp haven't survived the journey from Parris Island. "Don't pick your nose, asshole. Look like what you're supposed to be, not what you are!"

If war is confusion, so are exercises. After it is over, the NCOs and officers do their Monday morning quarterbacking. "One kid couldn't undo his seat belt," reports a staff sergeant who traveled with the troops. "Another couldn't do it up. Some of them had never flown in a helo before."

A tough captain who fought in Vietnam as an enlisted man isn't as upbeat as most of his superiors about the quality of contemporary marines. "We've got plenty of good leaders, good officers, and NCOs," he says, "but we need good followers, too. They may be more intelligent and better educated than they used to be, but it sure as hell takes just as long to train them. There are quite a few disciplinary problems at the School of Infantry such as people trying to duck out of it by saying they've got mental problems, or goofing off or falling asleep when they are supposed to be on fire watch. Three guys over at the other company refused to train the other day. Going on leave after boot camp before coming here is a big mistake. They come back twenty pounds overweight and look and sound like civilians again. They're supposed to be marines when they arrive, but I'm not so sure. Perhaps in a war they would shape up, but they don't give us instant obedience to orders down here."

Later, over a beer, a couple of staff NCOs who take their instructor jobs and the Marine Corps very seriously speak their minds. "What we need," says one, "is more 'chain' to train recruits and less officer supervision. The NCOs must also train the officers in the fleet and, in turn, learn from them. That's an important double link. The real danger now is that the new NCO corps may not be properly trained because a lot of us are looking over our shoulders too much of the time. Historically, good NCOs mean good troops—look at the British, the Germans, and the French Foreign Legion. You can't fuck up the NCOs and expect a good Marine Corps."

"There is a critique system here," says the other. "The students write comments on their NCO instructors for the company officers and staff, but they don't have to sign their papers. It's all very democratic but dangerous for the instructors' authority if these criticisms are taken too seriously. For example, I know a sergeant who had a student tell him that his cat had died at home. The sergeant told him to get another one. The student didn't like that. The sergeant asked how he would feel if his buddy in the next foxhole got a bullet between the eyes. The student complained to the chaplain that the sergeant was unsympathetic and insensitive and the sergeant was removed from his job as unit leader."

"Another problem," says the first speaker, "is that a lot of these new marines are promised that they will get barracks or sea duty after they have finished at the School of Infantry. When they come back to the fleet, they have forgotten all their infantry training."

"We hear that the new commandant has removed some of the supervising officers at Parris Island," says the other NCO. "It will be interesting to see if it happens here. The Marine Corps should get back to enlisted training enlisted. A lot of guys coming in today are looking for a job. They're not coming in to be a marine."

Old marines driving through the little town of Jacksonville might be surprised. The gunshops, pawnbrokers, tattoo parlors, the acres of used cars, and the ratio of ten males to every female haven't changed. But the bars have fallen on hard times. There is still a cluster of them outside Camp Geiger ("Dirty Harry," "Saigon Sam," etc.), but downtown Jacksonville is being cleaned up. A former battalion commander who was in Lejeune in the mid-1970s says he had more of his men absent without leave or in the brig than the whole of the Second Marine Division does today. Another officer remembers being on duty in those days and going downtown in a bus to pick up the stragglers from the bars. "I always took my .45 and it was strictly 'lock and load' after dark," he says. "There were a lot of wild and rough marines around then." One reason is that the minimum drinking age has been raised in the state from eighteen to twenty-one. Another is a much cleaner-living Marine Corps.

The amphibious assault vehicle, or "amtrac" to give it its old generic title, is almost as closely identified with the Marine Corps as the rifle. These are the tracked swimming vehicles that take the marines ashore from a mother ship. When a marine hits the beach, he hits it in an amtrac. The U.S.S. *Hermitage* is about three miles off Onslow Beach, waiting to launch the amtracs lined up in its well deck. The *Hermitage*, a twelve-thousand-ton landing ship dock can carry forty-five amtracs and three hundred marines, who spend six months on board ship in cramped quarters, where their bunks, or racks, are stacked four and sometimes six high.

The marines, looking sharp in their camouflaged utilities compared with the khaki uniforms of the navy, are stretched out on the top of the amtracs, standing around talking or drinking soda and spitting tobacco juice at the sparrows on the splintered wooden floor of the well deck. There is the camaraderie of a close-knit, professional, and happy unit doing its thing in the fleet. The captain commanding the company says there is less stiffness between the ranks here than on the drillfield or in the infantry school. The older NCOs, he says, get a "grip" on the young second lieutenants, and if the latter don't shape up, they move on.

A second lieutenant wearing regulation Marine Corps eyeglasses draws a chalk plan of the beach on the side of an amtrac. He shouts to make himself heard above the noise of the ship's engines. He talks of first and second waves, of the LOD, or line of departure, and asks his men if there are any questions. The captain stands by, listening. The *Hermitage* has slowed to three knots for the launch and is filling its ballast tanks with sea water to tilt the ship down at the rear so that the amtracs can roll off the stern gate of the well deck. The weather has taken a turn for the worse. Pewter-colored clouds are building up overhead. There is the distant boom of surf on the beach.

"Fifteen minutes to launch. Troops load," a metallic voice announces over the ship's public address system.

We climb into the rear amtrac. There is a three-man crew: troop commander, crew chief, and driver. Weighing twenty-six tons empty, the amtracs can carry up to eighteen fully equipped marines, though fifteen is more usual. The driver, who can get very wet, is wearing green overalls. "It's like being in a garbage bag," says a lieutenant. "Very, very hot."

We strap on life jackets that can be blown up by a carbon dioxide cartridge or manually inflated. There is also a "buddy line" cord. There are pontoons filled with air on each side of the amtrac, and the amphibian can wallow along at about seven or eight knots in the water. On land, they usually travel at a maximum speed of forty-five miles per hour but can go up to fifty-five if necessary. The armor stops .762 rounds but a .50 caliber machine gun bullet will rip through the aluminum-sided hull of the vehicle. It offers reasonable protection against shrapnel fragments and antipersonnel mines, but antitank mines can blow it to kingdom come.

Developed from the amtrac used in Vietnam, which had a gas fuel tank underneath and was highly vulnerable to mines—the marines used to put sandbags on the roof and ride up there—the latest version is diesel powered. Its real strength, however, is in the water. It can handle surf up to ten feet high, and its endurance in the water is only limited by fuel and the tolerance of the men inside. During some tests in fifteen feet of surf off Monterey, in California, an amtrac overturned twice but came up the right way and continued swimming to shore.

The amtracs slowly grind down the well deck to the stern. There is about a foot of water now where the ramp meets the sea. The cabin is hot, lit by a single feeble bulb, and there is a strong smell of diesel fumes.

"Go!" shouts the crew chief. The amtrac lurches and slithers, there is a splash, a momentary sinking sensation as water crashes in over the driver, who guns the engine, and then a much more comfortable bobbing motion.

"They're pretty safe," says a staff sergeant who is the section leader. "The most dangerous thing, apart from gunfire, is getting stuck on a sandbar or coral. You can sometimes lose your front sprockets that way and suddenly there's a big hole, and down you go." He tells of an accident off this coast not so long ago. The crew chief forgot to close the rear hatch and the amtrac sank like a stone in thirty-eight feet of water. The other two members of the crew got out quickly but the chief's clothing became caught up in the turret. However, he finally managed to disentangle himself, popped his carbon dioxide cannister, and shot up to the surface to tell the tale.

The amtracs slowly form into a column and bob and sway to the distant shoreline. Twin rooster tails from blowholes at the rear mark the progress of each vehicle. Every now and again, a heavy swell catches the amtrac and water sluices over the driver. The worst part is waiting around for everyone else to form up. Sitting there in the gloom and diesel stench, it is not hard to imagine what it would be like if this was for real with the naval gunfire roaring overhead, flashes from exploding shells glimpsed through the cracks in the turret, and the crash of mortars, artillery, and small arms coming from the shore.

You can more readily believe, after an hour of agonizingly slow progress, the old sea tale that the marines cheered as they hit the beaches in World War II not because they were gung ho and dying to get to grips with the enemy but because their ordeal in the amtracs was over. The thought also arises that marines haven't had to assault a seriously defended beach since the Korean War. What's all this in aid of anyway?

There is a thud as the amtrac makes contact with the beach. The driver barrels the engine and the vehicle churns up the strand, water pouring off every rivet and down every neck. What's the drill, just out of curiosity, if you are seasick?

"If you throw up," says a grunt, "you're supposed to do it in your helmet so the floor doesn't get slippery." Vomit running down your face as you hit the beach is clearly a lesser evil than a sloppy and potentially dangerous amtrac floor. John Wayne wouldn't have seen it that way, but then he never had to go to war in an amtrac.

Three faces of
training: Camp Lejeune
Following pages
Moving out
Amtracs: ready
to go from Onslow
Beach, and then
coming aboard
the U.S.S. *Hermitage*
Landing zone.
Troops practicing
a helicopter-borne assault
from CH-53s
at the School of
Infantry, Camp Lejeune

Okinawa, Japan

THE ROCK

Resembling a misshapen lizard or a sea horse, depending on your fancy, Okinawa is Japan's southernmost island and has been known to hundreds of thousands of marines as the Rock. Okinawa was the last Pacific island to be assaulted and conquered in World War II, the end of a string of bloody island victories against the Japanese. Two marine divisions waded ashore on April Fool's Day, 1945, and marines have been there ever since.

The ties with Okinawa were reinforced by a second war, when thousands of marines came to the island in transit to Vietnam. Most of them returned by the same route, some with their bodies—if not their psyches—intact. Others were wounded, maimed, or disabled, and the rest came back in body bags.

The irony is that this slender subtropical island (sixty-seven miles long but only nineteen miles at its widest point) is inhabited by the most pacific of people. The Okinawans, not really Japanese at all, have their origins in China, Korea, and Malaya. Conquered by the Japanese in 1875, they resisted the martial ways of mainland Japan. But in early 1945, the Japanese high command decided to make a do-or-die stand on the distant island to delay the Allied attack on Japan itself.

The battle for Okinawa was one of the most closely fought and protracted of the Pacific island campaigns. William Manchester, the writer, who was there as a sergeant in the Twenty-ninth Marine Regiment, vividly reproduces the grimness of the battle in an article in the *New York Times Magazine*.

The struggle for Sugar Loaf Hill [a key objective] lasted ten days; we fought under the worst possible conditions—a driving rain that never seemed to slacken, day or night. (I remember wondering, in an idiotic moment—no man in combat is really sane—whether the battle could be called off, or at least postponed, because of the bad weather.) Casualties were almost unbelievable. In the 22d and 29th Marine regiments, two out of every three men fell. The struggle for the dominance of Sugar Loaf was probably the costliest engagement in the history of the Marine Corps. But by early evening on May 18, as night thickened over the embattled armies, the 29th Marines had taken Sugar Loaf, this time for keeps.

The battle lasted almost three months. U.S. forces lost 12,500 men, and 37,500 were wounded; the Japanese defenders, numbering 73,000 men, were virtually wiped out or committed suicide; and 42,000 Okinawan civilians, including thousands of women and children, were killed. In an incident that Okinawans have never forgotten, some eighty student nurses threw themselves over a cliff to their deaths, rather than face what they had been told would be rape, torture, and dishonor at the hands of the American troops.

For all this, Okinawans blame the Japanese rather than their conquerors, with whom they are on remarkably good terms. To this day, the islanders bitterly resent Japan's decision to delay the attack on the mainland by sacrificing them. No Japanese flags fly over Okinawa except at Japanese Defense Force bases, and Japanese troops, unlike their American counterparts, are confined to their camps for the duration of their service on the island.

The marine presence is sizable (twenty-two thousand officers and enlisted, plus about seven thousand dependents), and Okinawa is as familiar to most marines as are Camps Lejeune and Pendleton. Virtually every marine serves here, usually a six-month or a one-year unaccompanied tour, although new housing and improved living conditions are making it possible for more families to come.

The island has great beaches, plenty of aquatic sports, mild winters, good Japanese food, and a friendly, hard-working local population. The downside consists of typhoons, broiling humidity-drenched summers, the venomous and nocturnal habu snake, very limited entertainment off base, and more used-car lots than urban America. There is also a seemingly endless journey from the U.S. that involves eighteen hours of flying and a disorienting loss of a day (from crossing the international date line), all of which produce a monumental week-long jet lag.

From the military point of view, there are good jungle training grounds in the north of the island, plenty of water and beaches for amphibious exercises, and some fine coral reefs that make life more interesting for amtrac drivers, who learn the hard way what it is like to be snagged on a coral growth half a mile from the shore.

The numerous American bases are so intensely American that, if it weren't for the jet lag, it would be hard to believe that you had left the States. On base, only the lack of fresh milk in the stores, the single TV channel, and the absence of radio and television commercials remind the visitor that he is somewhere else.

For liberty there are the usual bars, discos, and clip joints with imported Filipino girls. The biggest and most notorious district is Kin Village, conveniently situated directly outside the gate of Camp Hansen. For the lucky men who are married or who have partners, there are the more discreet delights of the "love motels." These are establishments where a luxurious suite can be rented by the hour. To ensure privacy and anonymity, everything, including the orders for drinks and food and delivery of the bill, is done by telephone or computer. Guests, who never see the staff, drive into a garage situated directly under their room but cannot leave—the garage door is locked electronically after they have entered—until they have sent their money down a hydraulic chute. These motels are primarily for Japanese couples desperate to have some time to themselves away from relatives and children in overcrowded houses and apartments, but foreigners make good use of them too.

SPECIAL OPERATIONS

Halfway up the east coast of Okinawa there is a marine base called Camp Schwab. Perched on a cliff overlooking the sea is a barn-size building, and in front of that stands a lieutenant colonel in camouflage utilities with a scuba badge and parachute jump wings on his chest. He is Wheeler Baker, a veteran reconnaissance marine who is now passing on his skills to countless others as the corps upgrades its special operations capability, or SOC in military shorthand.

Special operations covers many things. The eighteen designated skills that are taught include moving swiftly and surely at night without use of radios, blowing up enemy installations, performing mountain rescue operations, evacuating American nationals from an unfriendly foreign environment, and being proficient in hand-to-hand combat. The training also involves improved intelligence techniques and new equipment.

The decision to give ordinary marine infantry units specialized commando training seems to have sprung from the growth of terrorism and unconventional warfare around the world. Rivalry with the U.S. Army, which had begun to train its forces to do the same thing for the same reasons, may have also had something to do with it. All marine expeditionary amphibious units are being upgraded to make them capable of these kinds of special operations.

"All our training is done at night," says Lieutenant Colonel Baker. "Last night, for example, we had a company doing an amphibious raid. It started off at 8:00 P.M. and spent about five hours at sea. Reconnaissance swimmers went ahead to survey the beach. They signaled back to a security detachment using infrared lights, which can only be seen with special goggles. The security guys came in and set up a secure zone. Some of the amphibious assault vehicles got hung up for a bit on the coral, but the force eventually landed intact. The troops then had a three-hour march inland to the objective, a terrorist base camp that they 'attacked' with mortars and grenades. Three CH-53 helicopters lifted the company out at dawn."

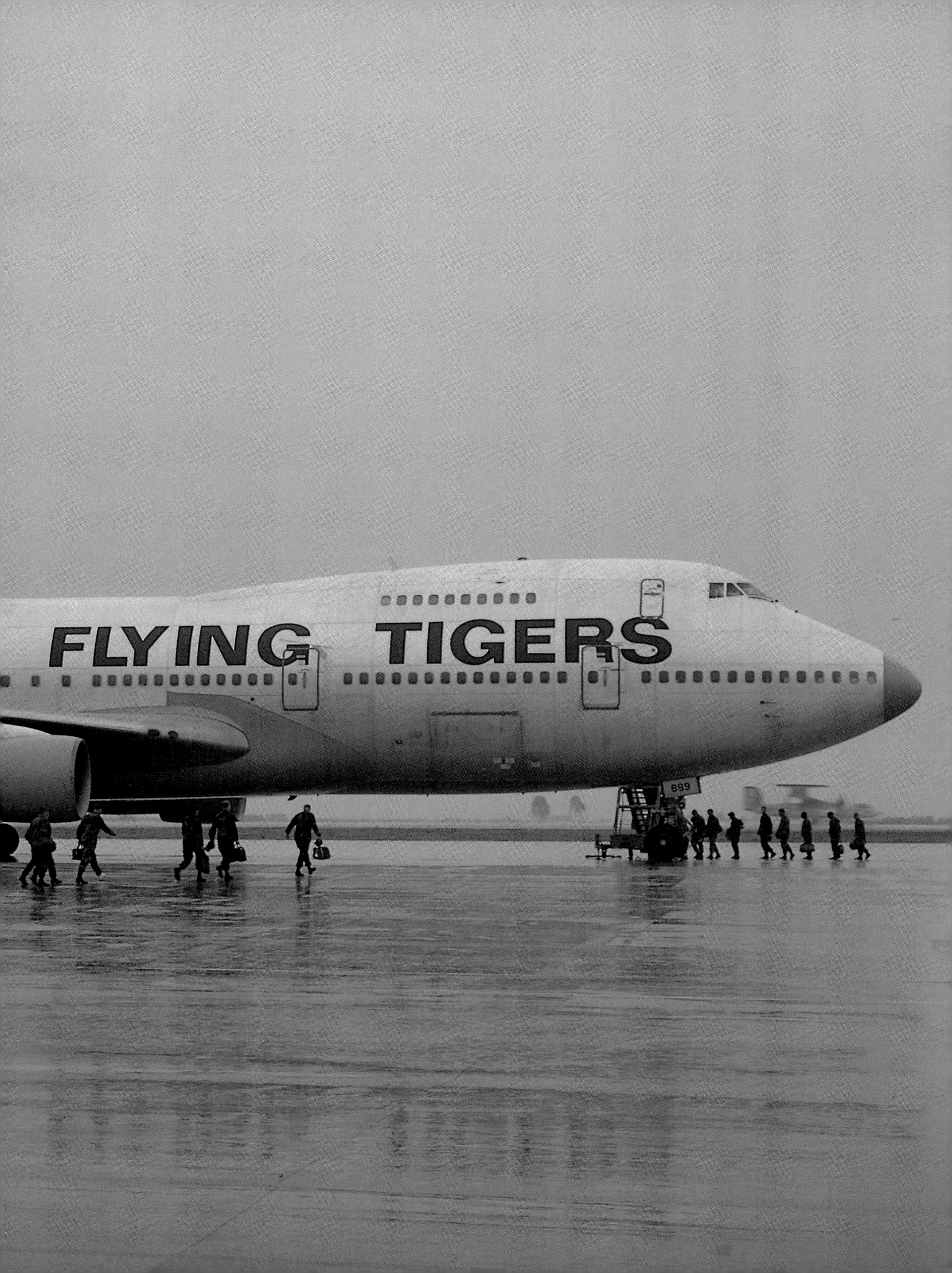
FLYING TIGERS

Joined by Captain Kelly McCann, the hand-to-hand combat, rappelling, and pistol expert who is clad in a green T-shirt and utility trousers, Wheeler Baker continues. "Our approach to training is very unglamorous, but it is realistic. If, for example, a company commander does not have a piece of equipment or a specialist that he needs at the beginning of an operation, he won't be able to get them later. We've also improved our radio communications. They've gone from the atrocious, when everyone seemed to talk all the time, to virtually no communications. The key thing is practice and repetition—that's where we make most of our money."

A couple of reconnaissance marines in wet suits are emerging from the blue-green water onto the beach, rather like the first amphibians to claw themselves out of the sea. Captain McCann walks to the edge of the fifty-foot cliff and demonstrates the latest state-of-the-art rappelling pack, which is tucked away in a small pouch that measures $8'' \times 4'' \times 2''$ and is fastened to his canvas web belt. A metal stake in the ground simulates a door handle or some other anchoring object in a building from which a marine might need to decamp in a hurry.

McCann, a compact though unspectacular figure for someone who packs so many lethal skills, unzips the pouch and pulls out a coil of light tubular nylon rope that has a tensile strength of forty-five hundred pounds. It is long enough to be used from the third story of a building. He passes the rope through a metal bracket on his belt and disappears over the side of the cliff. Forty-five seconds later he is on the beach, fifty feet below.

A little later, McCann is instructing marines in hand-to-hand combat in a gymnasium with a padded floor. The students will be used to "attack" the instructors who are undergoing their final test that evening before being sent back to their units to train others. Captain McCann will be explaining their role, but first he gives them some background to the Marine Corps' thinking on hand-to-hand combat.

"We believe in a very linear, direct style of fighting," he begins. "We don't go in for the circular stuff with its flowing, dancing kind of movement. There's no real mysticism or religion or philosophy. We don't walk on rice paper or learn to play flutes or anything like that. Our technique is very straightforward, very violent. Our motto is: the only dirty fight is the one you lose."

The Marine Corps' version of hand-to-hand combat has, McCann explains, three main sources. First, there was John Styers, who started training marines in the thirties, was later wounded on Iwo Jima, but continued instructing into the fifties. The second fellow who contributed to the package was Captain Bruce Fairburn, a Briton in the Shanghai Municipal Police who taught hand-to-hand combat in the twenties and thirties. His technique had a jujitsu base, a throwing and striking type of fighting.

The third system was developed by Colonel David Ben-Asher of the Israeli Defense Force. He started *krav-maga.* McCann explains that this is again a very direct "no bullshit" approach to fighting that is still taught in Israel. "Summing it up," says McCann, "I call ours the Styers technique because he is the granddaddy of it all.

"What we are trying to do with the marines," he says, "is to combine the techniques into one and teach it in a very short time—that is, three hours a day, three days a week for three weeks. We don't want to go through this really laborious process of stretching, learning philosophy, and all that nonsense. So we tossed out some of the acrobatics like high kicks, which are the kind of thing a normal person isn't capable of doing fast enough anyway. We want to use the things that normal people can do—punch, kick, blows to the body, grabs, and throws. We have tried to take the wrestling out of the fight. You try to make it so that the fight is over in five seconds, instead of wrestling on the ground and kicking. The whole point is to close in and get it over with so you can move on."

McCann, whose idea of a pleasant weekend is hanging over the cliffs in the

northern training areas or catching the poisonous habu snake for Okinawan mongoose fights (the going rate for a habu is $60), expounds on hand-to-hand combat. "In real life," he says, "I think you'll find that a fight starts most of the time not by someone staging it. Usually it's a blind-side attack. He's picked you as a target for whatever reason, and all of a sudden he is going to whistle into you. So we try to teach the student to do a bunch of different things.

"We work on a twenty-foot rule that puts the threats out at twenty feet. You can have your hands in your pockets, you can be smoking a cigarette, or having a drink. At fifteen feet, that's when your hands start to come out of your pockets and you get a bit more alert and watch where you are and what's going on around in the room. At ten feet your hands start coming up around your face, rubbing your nose and so on. At five feet, if it looks inevitable that he is coming at you, then you attack him. How can you be sure he's coming in? It's a gut feeling in the end, and it's a judgment call. You launch the attack and break his momentum and, hopefully, startle him."

McCann produces a shopping list of possible assaults. There are pistol attacks from the front, side, and rear; knife attacks in underhand, overhand, side-to-side, and slashing motions. There are kicks, being grabbed from behind and being run backward and punches of all kinds, including the simple sucker blow to the face.

"What we try to do with our system," McCann says, "is always make the initial response very defensive. But from there you move to the offensive. You protect yourself and from that a severely offensive move flows, a move that injures him. For example, you use elbows and knees if someone blind-sides you—you shorten the stick. If you try to punch someone when they are close into you, you lose a lot of power in the punch.

"With knife and pistol threats, the situation is very grave. You would first obviously try to get away from him if you could. If you can't, you need to control the weapon itself, then the hand that holds it, and finally the attacker himself. The best way to strike is an elbow to the head, a knee to the groin, a head butt—something they don't expect.

"You hear a lot of people talking about kicks—you know, 'I'd kick him, I'd kick him,'" McCann continues. "But they never do. People don't kick because they forget. They revert to what they have always been taught, which is grappling, wrestling, punching, or grabbing him and throwing him on the ground. What we try to do is to hurt him right up front and then grab him. You never want to grab someone who is unhurt because if he is stronger than you, he'll just kick your ass. But if you hurt him first then grab him, now you're in control of the situation.

"We use judo, jujitsu, and akido techniques but very little karate because it's mostly leg kicks. We only do one kick, a front snap kick, a very fast kick designed to hit from the groin down with the heel or ball of your foot. We train in bare feet so if they do it wrong, like a punt, they feel the pain."

McCann draws a distinction between pacifying and more lethal moves. "You judge that by the nature of the attack," he says. "A sober aggressor merits a much harsher response than a drunk whom we want to control but not necessarily hurt."

Marines are taught so they can fight anywhere, but the idea is also to build confidence, esprit de corps, and general toughness. "People join the Marine Corps to be tough, and that's what they do," says McCann. "They get hit in the head a couple of times, but that's the way it is. They're not afraid of it. The key is to throw a correct blow, not just haymakers, and to keep your cool when you are fighting so you don't revert to being a barnstormer."

Are the marines trying to kill people?

"In the right situation, we are," McCann replies. "If someone is trying to kill you, yes, you try to kill them. But the whole system makes you less apt to fight because you really see what you can do. You have a quiet confidence, and you're more likely to beg out of a fight than get into one."

Does he worry that someone might abuse these skills?

The captain thinks for a moment. "No, not really," he says, "because even though you learn a technique, the bottom line is if you go looking for trouble you're always going to find more than you can handle. Sure, you can be an instructor, you can be the best there is, but there's always another guy who can kick your ass. The minute you start thinking you're Billy Bad Ass, you'll get into trouble. I do worry about someone using it in a bully fashion on someone weaker. But if a guy is out there trying to turn it on people bigger and stronger routinely, he may be good at it, all right. But sooner or later he'll meet his match."

Does the bigger guy always win in the end?

"I don't believe that," says McCann, who is not a big guy himself. "I think the small guys can win through speed — speed scares people — through ferocity, and I think they can win through skill."

McCann has some interesting thoughts on the marines as an institution. "The Marine Corps likes charismatic and credible people," he says. "If you have these two qualities, the corps will let you move upward. It's a basic premise that you do things by the book, but after that you take risks. All great warriors were artists in laying their asses out. They all took risks, calculated risks. But it's a funny place. Sometimes we eat our own; other times it's a very endearing place to be. Marines will always do well in combat, possibly for the wrong reasons. We have an obligation to the American people to keep the Marine Corps romantic, and you do that by being tough. We'll always push harder. The thing we have going for us over the other services is *heart*."

Beaufort, South Carolina

The sun is out on a fine spring day for the change of command ceremony at the Marine Corps Air Station, near Beaufort (and Parris Island), South Carolina. Serried ranks of F/A 18 Hornet fighters, silvery gray with their distinctive twin tails, form a backdrop for the parade. Pride of place is given to two veterans, an F-4 Phantom and an A-4 Skyhawk, which are both being retired either to the Marine Corps Reserve or to a military boneyard in Arizona.

The transition from Phantom to Hornet is complete at Beaufort, and the commander, a bird colonel, is handing over command. There is a band, marching marines, a small crowd of wives, mothers, children, and friends. There are also speeches of a predictable and, to civilian ears, a rather old-fashioned kind. The outgoing commander says: "On the surface there is pomp and circumstance whereas below lies the iron reality of accountability"; and, a little later, "Amazing grace, that's what keeps us alive"; and, "The sound of fighters taking off is the sound of freedom," and, finally, "The United States is worth fighting for and worth dying for."

In the pilots' ready room, Major Bob Watts, a former Phantom pilot who converted to Hornets, adds flesh to the notion of "iron accountability." Gesticulating with a tiny model of a Hornet on a stick, he talks about flying this most modern of fighters. "It's more like handling a skateboard than a bike. Once you've learned a straight run, you don't forget it. But if you want to do tricks, you've got to do them every day. In this business you don't have the luxury of a couple of weeks to get up to speed. We advertise that we are ready to go at moment's notice, so we have to train every day. And we are ready."

With modern electronics every detail of a training "hop" can be examined, discussed, and evaluated. Through a device that looks like a gunsight affixed to the windshield, the pilot can keep a constant check on air speed, altitude, distance, fuel,

Fuselage detail
of an F/A 18
Hornet fighter:
Marine Corps Air
Station,
Beaufort, South
Carolina
Detail of a
fighter pilot's
flight suit
Scale models
of Soviet and other
enemy'' aircraft
Major Bob
Watts, Hornet
pilot and operations
officer of 122
Squadron (Crusaders),
demonstrating
tactics
Following pages
Change of
command ceremony
on the flight
line: Beaufort

and other data without moving his head. There are three other screens in the cockpit as well as a bewildering selection of dials, switches, buttons, and wires. It's odd that after this complexity it appears that the nose cap of the Hornet is held on by a single diminutive Phillips screw. (It's difficult not to wonder what would happen if it were taken off.)

And then there's Bitching Betty, a talking computer which is probably related to Hal in Stanley Kubrick's film *2001: A Space Odyssey.* "She always talks when you're busy or someone else is talking to you on the radio," says Watts. Betty has a limited but arresting vocabulary. She says things like: "Flight controls! Flight controls!" "Fuel low!" "Flameout! Flameout!" (One of your engines has quit.) "Bingo! bingo!" (You've got just enough fuel to get back to base, so hurry.) "She's a bitch all right," says Watts, "but I wouldn't be without her. It helps to have someone tell you, 'Hey, your engine is on fire. You'd better do something about it, pal.'"

Watts, who flew on the exercise in Norway and whom we met yet again in the Philippines, stresses the versatility of this "video" jet and its maneuverability in aerial combat. He picks up a model of the latest Soviet MiG fighter and demonstrates some of the tactics. Evading an intercept by rolling quickly and turning into the attacker can be handled comfortably by the aircraft but puts considerable strain on the pilot. Gravity pressure can go from normal (1 G) to six times that pressure (6 G's) in less than a second during such a maneuver. Hornet pilots wear a "G-suit," which is a kind of padded overall filled with compressed air that helps to restrict the flow of blood from the head to the feet, the phenomenon that occurs during aerobatic maneuvers that can produce blackouts. When the G's mount, pilots grunt, groan, and even scream to help keep the blood up where it should be. Hornets are governed to a maximum of 7½ G's, but the air force's F-16 Eagles have gone up to 9 G's; there, as Watts says, the lights go out quickly, and planes and pilots have been lost.

Watts describes what it is like taking off from an aircraft carrier. When the aircraft is hooked up to the catapult, the pilot puts his left hand on the throttle, arm extended rigid. His right hand goes on the "Jesus" handle. The vital thing is not to touch the stick. The sensation when the catapult is fired, says Watts, is like a bucking bronco, a sudden jolting leap in the air.

Between the pilot's legs in the Hornet is a large ring, the only ring in the cockpit. This is the "Jesus" handle. The pilot reaches down and pulls it only when he is in deep trouble. A quick tug fires the ejection seat two hundred feet into the air. There have been cases of civilians, and even pilots, who have accidentally pulled the ring while sitting on the ground, usually with fatal results. According to Watts, the safest speed at which to eject, if you have the luxury of choosing, is about three hundred knots. "At about four hundred knots, your limbs start to flail," he says, "and above five hundred knots the wind will kill you." Unfortunately, aerial combat is mostly at the higher speeds thus markedly reducing the chances of a pilot's survival if he had to eject.

The Marine Corps' air wing has pretty neat gear. Apart from the macho leather flight jacket and the leather wings stitched onto the normal flight suit uniform, only marines serving in aviation wear patches identifying them by name and unit. The ground marine is a very anonymous individual by comparison. For pilots, there are many additional, if largely functional, items that include a forty-pound torso harness, the space age helmet and visor (with a piece of soft chamois for cleaning the visor), a life vest that activates itself when it makes contact with water, a Swiss army knife, and some rather fine-looking flight gloves ("So your hands don't stay on the airplane in a place like Norway," says Watts, "or burn in the desert.")

One thing, however, has not changed in the combat flying business. Bob Watts always carries with him a can of water, sealed in 1940, and an antisnakebite kit to protect the plane from being "bitten," or jinxed. Old-fashioned superstition is alive and well in state-of-the-art marine aviation.

Jet intake of A-6 Intruder: Cherry Point, North Carolina
Following pages
One of the marines' last great F-4 Phantom fighter bombers taxiing: El Toro, California
Crew chief's parting salute, returned by Hornet pilot in the cockpit
Hot end of the Hornet

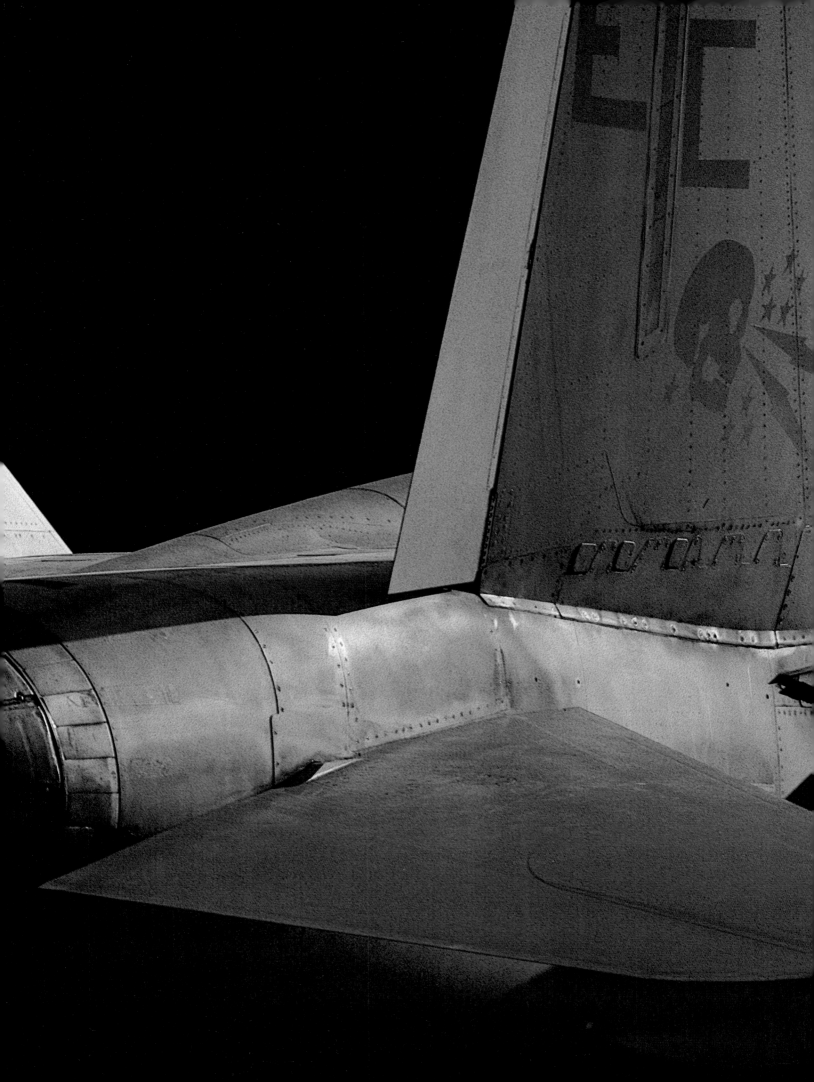

Someone who had known parade fields, barracks that
shone with polish and pride, firm-faced men older than their years
who starched their utilities,
shined their boots, and shaved their heads.

AN OLD-STYLE STAFF NCO IN *FIELDS OF FIRE* BY JAMES H. WEBB

PART 3:
THE
BARRACKS

Following pages
Ceremonial rifle
platoon at port arms:
Marine Barracks,
Washington, D.C.

Marine Barracks, Washington, D.C.

MARINES ON PARADE

The small patch of turf surrounded by some old but undistinguished buildings in a corner of southeast Washington could easily be overlooked by a casual visitor to the city. Usually referred to as "8th and I Streets," its geographic boundaries, or by the simple title Marine Barracks, the place has none of the resonance of the capital's other historic sites. It isn't even the headquarters of the corps.

Yet this is hallowed real estate for the marines. It is the oldest post of the corps, the stage for the marines' marching and musical spectaculars—the finest martial performances of their kind in America—and the home of the commandant and the Marine Band.

Eighth and "Eye," as generations of marines have called it, has been the physical and spiritual home of the Marine Corps since the damp, cold March day in 1801 when President Thomas Jefferson and Lieutenant Colonel William Ward Burrows, then commandant, rode out of the city to look for a suitable spot for a barracks for the marines and a home for their commandant.

The barracks underwent the vicissitudes of fire and demolition, but the commandant's house, a large brick building in the Federalist style at the north end of the parade ground, survived. Spared by the British in their sacking of Washington in 1814, it has been the home of every commandant except the first two. It is, by all accounts, the oldest continually occupied public residence in Washington.

It is a balmy summer's evening now, and the commandant and his wife are receiving their guests in the garden. The setting is a pleasurable assault on the senses: dark green foliage contrasts with a scarlet and gold tent (Marine Corps colors) and the glint of multicolored medal ribbons on crisp white uniforms; the perfumes of elegant bare-armed women mingle with the pungency of sizzling canapes and the dusty scent of roses and hyacinths.

A small jazz combo from the Marine Band plays in one corner as generals, admirals, politicians, and other power brokers of the capital file into the garden. The Vice-President of the United States works the crowd, vigorously shaking hands. The chairman of the Joint Chiefs of Staff, two Navy Secretaries (past and incumbent), the head of the CIA, and many grizzled former marines stand in line to meet their hosts.

An aerial reconnaissance report of the scene would depict it as just another starchy gathering of Washington's glitterati. But the worm's-eye view is different. There is a comfortable, easygoing camaraderie, a sense of family that is unusual. There is a lot of banter and laughter, some boisterous reunions ("Son of a gun, where in the hell have you been?"), and some new-corps-isn't-like-the-old-corps comparisons. "They don't seem to have any fun these days," complained a retired Korean War veteran. "They should laugh more."

Yet this is a very special occasion, as important to marines as a presidential inauguration is to the citizenry, an event that also recurs every four years. Tonight is the "change of command" ceremony; the moment when one commandant replaces another. The king is dead; long live the king.

Young marine officers and NCOs, immaculate in blue-whites dress, offering their arms to the ladies, escort the guests to their seats in the stands that line two sides of the parade ground. There is a large, expectant crowd in the bleachers as the lights go down, leaving only the afterglow of a hot summer's day and the gleam of lamps suffused by lace curtains in the windows of the commandant's house.

The ceremony follows a pattern similar to the regular Friday evening parades held throughout the summer. A rich mellifluous voice, belonging to a marine sergeant who has been specially chosen for the job, provides a commentary throughout the show. It begins with a concert given by the United States Marine Band. Marches by John Philip Sousa, who once led the band and left his indelible stamp on it, dominate the program, although Irving Berlin makes an appearance with his "God Bless America" sung in a fine baritone by a member of the band.

There are honors for the Vice-President. The audience stands, officers salute, and the band plays ruffles and flourishes followed by a tune. I lean over and ask a general about the tune. He shakes his head and says that it must be the Vice-President's "own little ditty." (It turns out to be "Hail Columbia.")

Under floods and spotlights that would not disgrace Broadway, the pageant unfolds. Shadowy figures can be seen behind the shrubbery in the arcade that faces the stands; there are hoarse commands and the clash of hands on rifles; the band strikes up "Colonel Bogey," a piece of martial music that always seems to raise the hair on the back of one's neck, even if it also resurrects the image of Alec Guinness looking horrified at the prospect of blowing up his beloved bridge over the river Kwai.

The troops march on and form up in front of the stands on the far side of the "parade deck." "Order Arms!" There are swift synchronized moves with the precision—and satisfaction—of a sports car's gears meshing into place at high speed. Then comes a crunching crash as 150 rifle butt plates hit the asphalt. From a section of the grandstand occupied by staff NCO's and brand-new second lieutenants from Quantico comes a burst of cheering mixed with a peculiarly marine grunt of approval: "ARRUGAH!"

Heads swing upward to the parapet above the barracks. Nine buglers in scarlet blouses and white trousers, underlit, sound a fanfare . . . colors are presented, with the Color Guard moving like clockwork toy soldiers in 8th and I's special snake-hipped style of marching . . . the band, led by the drum major in a British bearskin, marches one way across the parade ground to "York'scher," a marvelous military melody by Beethoven . . . the Drum and Bugle Corps, full of punch and panache, marches in the other direction belting out "Scotland the Brave" and "Minstrel Boy."

There is much movement; incomprehensible orders are shouted followed by copious saluting. Then the Drum and Bugle Corps comes on for its concert. The instrumentation is more complex than it sounds. The horn line consists of bugles ranging from soprano to contrabass. The percussion section features snare drums, timpani, bass drums, and instruments officially called "marching xylophones." There are two of these carried with a metal contraption around each player's neck, resembling nothing so much as two marines in dress blues and neck braces, marching in step carrying a couple of barbecue grills. In the band are several women, two very small with faces barely visible under their hats.

The buglers whip their instruments to their lips as if they have been stung, the spotlights close in, and the concert begins. The repertoire is eclectic. There is a patriotic song, an operatic piece, a drum solo, and a rousing conclusion with "America the Beautiful." The band has a jazzy, modern sound that would not be out of place at a college football game. The crowd loves it.

The colors—that is, the national flag and the Marine Corps battle colors with its honor streamers commemorating battles fought all over the world, the men who died, and the victories won—are brought forward. With a reverence that is almost religious, the colors are handed over by the retiring commandant to his successor, symbolizing a change of command that has occurred twenty-eight times in the past two hundred years. The two men take turns to speak, to look backward, and to look forward, to praise, to exhort, to reflect.

The Vice-President delivers a eulogy (what else would he do?) and the troops pass in review to the marines' own little ditties: Sousa's "Semper Fidelis" and "The Marine Corps Hymn." After the march past, the retiring commandant's wife joins him

reviewing stand and they remain there, holding hands under the lights as the music fades away.

The crowd remains seated and silent; the light continues to glow from the house the couple has lived in for the past four years. This is his last day as a United States Marine, his last day as commandant, the last day when he and his wife can call the oldest post in the corps "home."

Who knows what they are thinking or feeling, but the crowd seems to understand and experiences a moment of collective empathy for the marine who was a god just a few minutes ago and who, as the bittersweet sound of taps tingles in the membranes, is now a mere mortal.

THE UNITED STATES MARINE BAND

The office of Colonel John R. Bourgeois, director of the band, is like a museum, a museum primarily dedicated to John Philip Sousa, the legendary March King, seventeenth director of the band and the patriarch of American military music. Sousa's baton is on display in a glass case, "the orb and scepter" of the band, says Bourgeois. It rarely emerges from its shrine but is used for the ceremonial handover from one director to another.

In front of the colonel's desk is a magnificent blue and green Tiffany standard lamp that also belonged to the great man. The lamp casts light on a photograph of the band, taken in 1865, that included three drummer boys. A closer look reveals a small child near the bearded trombonists. Sousa's father was a trombonist in the band. Was the boy at his feet his talented son? Everyone likes to think so, but no one is sure.

The band is a rather odd and rather special part of the Marine Corps. It owes its first allegiance not to the corps but to the President of the United States and is known as The President's Own. "The Marine Corps is tradition and so is the band, the keeper of the flame," says Bourgeois. "We are America's version of the court musicians. Our sole mission is to provide music for the President."

Members of the band do not go through boot camp, and the only military training they receive is in marching and military etiquette at Marine Barracks. "We are noncombatant," says Bourgeois with a wisp of a smile, "to be prized and perhaps captured but not shot."

The band, led by five officers, is 143 musicians strong. To enter, the candidate auditions and, if successful, joins the band with the rank of staff sergeant. Women have been in the band since the early seventies; all auditions are done behind a screen lest what is seen warps judgment of what is heard. Vacancies are few since the band boasts a 90 percent re-enlistment rate.

The band has a distinctive, indeed unique, uniform. Members wear scarlet blouses; their blues trousers have a white stripe within the standard red stripe. NCO's chevrons enclose a music lyre instead of crossed rifles or an exploding bomb. The director wears a deep navy blue—in effect, black—coat. The drum major, the peacock of all military bands, is a law unto himself: in common with British Guards officers, his bearskin comes from the female of the species but still weighs four pounds when dry. The scarlet sash, or baldric, that goes across his scarlet blouse is encrusted with the gold letters of the Marine Corps battle honors, two drumsticks, The President's Own, and his personal decorations.

He has a standard staff NCO belt and sword but is the only enlisted man in the corps to wear an officer's belt buckle and globe and anchor emblems. His mace, made from malacca cane, is gold-plated and weighs a little over six pounds. It is embellished with the Capitol's dome, the corps' battle honors, the presidential seal, and the Marine Corps emblem. Bearskin, baldric, and mace are made in Britain.

Cold weather can make handling the mace difficult. And the answer to most spectators' unasked question about what does the fella do if he drops it is simple: he

General Paul X. Kelley, twenty-eighth commandant
Following pages
Garden party at the commandant's residence, Marine Barracks. General P.X. Kelley, retiring commandant, and General Alfred M. Gray, Jr., his successor, and their wives on the receiving line
Top brass
A family affair for the corps. Washington's glitterati gather at the garden party before the commandant's change of command ceremony on a balmy summer's evening

picks it up. A high wind poses problems in the upper rigging. The wind treats the bearskin like a sail—one that, rain or shine, seems to get heavier as the parade goes on.

The band has always been primarily a concert band; 95 percent of its activity is off the parade ground. Under Sousa, director from 1880 until 1892, the band started touring and has done so ever since. A typical year will include about six hundred U.S. and Canadian engagements.

The band recently made its first foreign tour to Holland at the invitation of the Marine Band of the Royal Netherlands Navy. There would be more foreign travel if the band had its own funds, but there is no budget for it. The Dutch tour was paid by the host country.

The President's Own is the oldest symphonic military band in America and was established by an act of Congress on July 11, 1798. It began as a drum and fife band but had added oboes, clarinets, French horns, and a bassoon by the time it played for Thomas Jefferson's inauguration. Jefferson, whose many talents included musical skills, is reputed to have given the band its presidential name, and the band has played at every inauguration since.

The director is the President's music adviser and plans the musical programs for inaugurations and White House functions. The band's first loyalty to the President is a serious matter. No matter how important an engagement may be, it will be summarily cancelled if there is conflict with a request from the White House. When the band tours, a substantial number of the musicians stay in Washington to look after the President's and the Marine Corps' musical needs.

Legislation forbids any commercial use of the band; expenses on tour are paid by local sponsors, and any profits go to charitable causes. The band does, however, make a few records, but these are for in-house consumption only. Ironically, it made some of the earliest records in the United States. The Columbia Phonograph Company released sixty cylinders recorded by the band, under Sousa, in the fall of 1890.

The band's library at Marine Barracks has more than forty thousand titles and is probably the most extensive band library in the world, according to Colonel Bourgeois. There is no doubt about the quality of the musicians, who are equally at home on the White House lawn; playing for the President and his guests at dinner; doing their annual gig at the Kennedy Center; or braving the cold and rain at the Iwo Jima Memorial and the Arlington National Cemetery. Their versatility ranges from the staple diet of Sousa and other marches to opera (there is a baritone singer who doubles as a narrator when needed), symphonic music, Broadway melodies, and even to jazz. The band can, in short, play almost anything, and play it well.

The music and the personality of Sousa live on. Although the band's heritage is European, there is a lot more swing to Sousa's marches and to American march music in general, though they are not necessarily faster. "We adapt from each other," says Bourgeois. "The military capture territory and installations, and bands sometimes capture music. That's a great British tradition, but we do it, too. We've captured Beethoven [the York'scher march], you might say."

Some critics believe the band's musical diet is too conventional: for instance, the same marches are played over and over at the Friday night parades and other military rituals. But Colonel Bourgeois believes in tradition.

"This band has to have a sense of history as well as music," he says. "Our brothers, the Drum and Bugle Corps, are more of a changing unit than we are. Although we play contemporary music, in concert our instruments haven't changed. For example, we keep both cornets and trumpets. Of course, we maintain a repertoire of dance music and backing for entertainers at the White House, but we've always done that. We are very much traditionalists and are proud of it."

And as a preserver of tradition, Colonel Bourgeois is careful to brief incoming commandants that they should never refer to this ancient entity as the "Marine Corps Band," as if they own it. It is, he says gently but firmly, the *United States Marine Band.*

THE UNITED STATES MARINE DRUM AND BUGLE CORPS

This group of musicians does not have the same lineage as the band. It was only established in 1934 at the suggestion of a Captain Lemuel Shepherd, a First World War veteran who was then captain of the guard at Marine Barracks and who later became commandant. But its spirit goes back to the early days of fife and drum, as old as the Marine Corps itself.

The Drum and Bugle Corps at the 8th and I Barracks, seventy-five musicians strong, with two small field units based in Georgia and California, are the only active duty bands of their kind left in the American military. The unit, however, shows no signs of joining the dinosaur. With its technical skills and its show-biz flair it continues to be an enormously popular crowd pleaser wherever it marches and plays.

Major Truman W. Crawford has been its director for more than two decades, but he had two other careers before joining the marines. For ten years he served in the U.S. Air Force Drum and Bugle Corps (now defunct) and then ran a music store catering to the needs of civilian bands. The United States Marine Drum and Bugle Corps is his life, and he leads it with zest, giving new meaning to the concept of job satisfaction.

The major's office, which is in a different wing of the barracks from the U.S. Marine Band, has the air of a musical recording studio. There is a piano, piles of sheet music scattered around, and a large number of cassettes sitting on his desk. Work is in hand for a television show in a week's time. On the walls are pictures of the original Drum and Bugle Corps formed on November 9, 1934, and of The Commandant's Own, as the corps is now known, performing at the dedication of the Iwo Jima Memorial in 1955. From somewhere down the corridor comes an explosion of drums. A sign on the major's desk admonishes: PRACTICE DOES NOT MAKE PERFECT. PERFECT PRACTICE MAKES PERFECT.

"I am a contemporary traditionalist," Major Crawford says. "In our parades and concerts we have things that go back to the 1700s, but we also play modern music. We are proud traditionalists, but we keep abreast of what is going on musically today and is of interest to young Americans."

The corps switches from one idiom to the other frequently and effortlessly. For example, one week may bring a highly traditional change of command ceremony and the next a television assignment celebrating two hundred years of American music in which the corps will be playing in support of such entertainers as Barbara Mandrell, Frankie Avalon, and the New City Singers.

But has the Drum and Bugle Corps gone too far in its desire to please modern audiences and to provide variety for its talented musicians? Has it turned into a hybrid, a sort of military high school band, as some critics allege? Major Crawford denies the charges. "Our instrumentation hasn't really changed in fifteen years. We have found a basic musical format and instrumentation that gives us the amount of flexibility we need for ceremony as well as television performances. We do not use any modern electronic devices, nor any type of amplification."

The biggest difference, he continues, is in the percussion section. In addition to the innovation of two marching xylophones, there are four different-size bass drums with different pitches. That means they not only provide the big bass "boom" that supports marching troops, but they can also be used melodically in a way that enhances the overall musical effect.

"You will also see drummers with three drums on the same harness," the major continues. "This produces visual impact with the stick work, as well as melodic and harmonic nuances that make the music more interesting. People talk about the xylophones, but they come from the tradition of the glockenspiel, a part of military marching music for generations."

The corps' instrumentation includes the basic snare drum, three tri-toms—essentially tom-toms that are pitched at different intervals—four tuned bass drums, and three cymbal players, who add a lot of flash and flair and visual color.

The brass section consists of soprano bugles similar in sound and timbre to a trumpet, mellophone bugles with the same timbre as a French horn, bass baritone bugles providing the voice of the trombone or baritone horn in a conventional concert or marching band, and contrabass bugles, which are like a Sousaphone yet still technically a bugle with the giant bell carried on the shoulder. All these instruments, whatever their size and sound, are two-valve piston bugles.

Unlike the United States Marine Band, the Drum and Bugle Corps recruits young men and women with proven musical skills straight out of high school and sends them to boot camp to be trained as any other marine. "They must complete recruit training," says Major Crawford. "They are marines in every sense of the word."

Then they go to Little Creek, Virginia, to the Naval School of Music for five months. "We don't teach them how to play," the major says, "but we refine their skills and post them to the field units or to the barracks after their training."

Mix the activities of a company of touring actors with the spring training of a major league baseball team and you have the flavor of a typical year in the life of the Drum and Bugle Corps. The musicians migrate to warmer climes (Arizona or Texas) in the spring for an intensive preparation for the summer season. The Silent Drill Platoon and the Color Guard accompany the corps, and intensive training—seven days a week for three weeks—begins.

"Tryout" time is next: they spend eight days on the West Coast testing old and new routines on live audiences, much like a Broadway show. Then they go back to Washington at the end of March. April is spent crisscrossing the country, performing constantly. The summer parades in the capital begin late in May and run until early September, but the musicians continue to tour on weekends. "It is not unusual to finish the Friday night parade, muster here at 6:00 A.M. on Saturday, and fly off to some distant place, returning on Sunday night," says Major Crawford.

In September a new touring phase begins with visits to places like Nashville and then on to Parris Island and other marine bases. Much of this is "in-house" marching and musical displays for marines and their families. But not all. There is, for instance, a three-week stint at the Dallas State Fair in the fall.

November sees the corps back in Washington for the Marine Corps birthday season. The final gig is a curious one: the Drum and Bugle Corps goes to Cuba to help keep up the spirits of the small marine detachment at the U.S. naval base at Guantanamo Bay. "An interesting place," says Major Crawford. "It's hard to be so close to America and yet so far way. A remote posting to say the least."

There are occasional foreign tours, but the summer obligations in Washington mean that concurrent events in Europe are difficult to attend. The corps has, however, been to Australia a couple of times in the winter. The Drum and Bugle Corps packs its instruments away at the beginning of December and the musicians take a month's leave as a unit.

The same rules that prevent the United States Marine Band from making commercial records and tapes apply to the Drum and Bugle Corps. Thus to hear them you have to see them, which isn't a bad idea anyway. Similarly, the corps cannot charge for public performances, though it can play at such events as college football games, which enhance the marines' image and recruiting.

The name The Commandant's Own came by accident. President Eisenhower was having dinner with the commandant and reminded him jokingly that the Marine Band belonged to him, not to the general. The commandant agreed, but on the spur of the moment said he didn't mind because he had the Drum and Bugle Corps. The title stuck.

Connoisseurs of marching bands remark on the contrast between American and European military bands. "The British, for example, have stayed staunch traditionalists," says Major Crawford. "They are playing as they did thirty years ago—the same instruments, the same repertoire, the same methodology. We feel we maintain the

Top left
Colonel Donald J. Myers, commanding officer, 8th and I Marine Barracks
Top right
Colonel John R. Bourgeois, director of the United States Marine Band, The President's Own
Bottom left
Master Sergeant Gary A. Petersen, drum major of the U.S. Marine Band
Bottom right
Master Gunnery Sergeant James L. Marcil, drum major of the USMC Drum and Bugle Corps, The Commandant's Own
Following page
The U.S. Marine Band, with ceremonial detachment, renders the last honors at Arlington Cemetery; officers' swords have black mourning knots on their hilts

tradition but supplement it with a tasteful amount of contemporary idiom to keep track with America. There is a difference, therefore, in pace, timbre, character. You can pick out a British group from fifty different bands. They have a very traditional brassy sound that has remained the same for decades.

"Our signature is an emotional involvement. Our programs have something for all—old, young, traditional, and contemporary. Nothing is mechanical or routine; we try to reach out to an audience. Whereas a British band, whose performance is academically very sound and well defined, does not tug at your emotions in the same way. Our success lies in the emotional impact we have on our listeners."

BEHIND THE SCENES

It is 7:40 A.M. on a misty Friday morning at 8th and I, the last day of the summer parade season. The marines are on the grass "parade deck" in their Charlies (khaki short-sleeved shirts, green trousers). The Color Guard is lining up in front of the 40mm naval cannons that are fired on such rare occasions as a state visit or the performance of Tchaikovsky's "1812 Overture." The colors in the old barracks—red brick, green turf, white belts and gloves—are subdued, softened by the gray sky and silvery mist.

"Attent-huh! Order-huh! Present-huh! Order-huh!" The Color Guard goes through its routine for the umpteenth time. The small son of a gunnery sergeant watches intently.

"What are they doing, Daddy?"

"Practicing, son. And what does practice do?"

"Makes perfect, Daddy."

One of the two rifle companies involved in ceremonial duties is on the parade ground practicing "Fix Bayonets," the most difficult drill routine of all, and some of the marines look a bit shaky. NCOs and company officers move up and down, criticizing, adjusting, clucking, encouraging, squinting, reprimanding.

The band comes on and plays the national anthem and "The Marine Corps Hymn"; a small group of civilians has gathered at the south end of the barracks to watch the dress rehearsal; five men in black shorts and green PT shirts take the flagpole down and march off with it; another group emerges and places small Marine Corps guidons at strategic points around the parade ground. There is the penetrating buzz of a hedge trimmer at work somewhere—all the barracks' hedges get a "high and tight" trim for the Friday evening parade; the U.S. flag is hoisted at the south end, and the troops disappear into the cloisterlike arcade for a break.

The main function of the 1,100 or so marines at 8th and I is to provide the ceremonial face of the Marine Corps, notably the evening parade every Friday at the barracks and the sunset parade every Tuesday at the Iwo Jima Memorial through the summer months. There are other "shots," or ceremonies, such as White House functions, military funerals, wreath layings at Arlington Cemetery, and joint ceremonial events with the other armed services.

The barracks also provides personnel for the White House, including an official "door opener" for the Oval Office; the Marine Corps Institute that is the corps' correspondence school; and such operational roles as guards for Camp David and contingency missions for the White House and the U.S. Capitol. One of those missions is riot control, a task that dates back to the 1800s but one that involved marines as recently as the late 1960s during the riots in Washington's ghettoes.

"There's a lot of pressure," says a senior officer, "but this is in many ways the Marine Corps' Vatican, and we get a lot of good people coming in here. What's special about this place is that it is our original post. We've held it ever since through war, invasion, fire, insurrection, race riots, and so on. This has been our place.

"We're the people charged with putting the best foot forward for the Marine Corps, whether it is the change of command for the commandant, a presidential inauguration, or the burial of a former private first class, who might have only been in the marines for a couple of years, in some civilian cemetery fifty miles from here.

"We have to give people who come to watch the Friday evening parades, whoever they are, a perfect performance. So when a lady wearing a size 16 stretch trou or a pink jump suit comes up to the main gate, we treat her just like the admiral's wife, the senator's wife, or the ambassador's wife who enters through the front door of the commandant's house. She must be accorded the same grace, courtesy, and interest. This may be the only time people have contact with the United States Marine Corps, and we must leave them with a good taste in their mouths."

And the "Hollywood" factor?

"Sure, there is a touch of Hollywood in the parade," says the same officer. "One colonel installed a fan to make sure that the flag, when it came down in limp and humid weather, would always be fluttering in the 'breeze.' But a general saw it and said that it was too much Hollywood, and that was the last week for the fan."

Not every marine can be posted to 8th and I. (Not every marine wants to be posted to there.) For the marching companies there is a height requirement: marines have to be between 5'11" and 6'2". The four-man Color Guard is even more restrictive, for giants only. While it may be difficult to get a posting, once there it is generally regarded as good for an individual's career curve. "It gives them a certain panache, polish, and perspective, for the most part healthy," says a senior officer. "It's also a nice place to be."

Over in a squad bay in a modern tower block across the road from the barracks, the marines are getting ready for the parade. They have been up since 5:30 that morning, have completed two rehearsals, and have eaten three square meals (What's the food like? "Hot chow's hot, cold chow's cold," says a lance corporal who is cleaning his shoes with the attention that women devote to their nails.). Having had a break in the afternoon, it is now 6:00 P.M., and backstage serious preparations are taking place.

You don't just get dressed for a ceremonial parade in the Marine Corps. Putting on the distinctive blue and white uniform is a ritual, done with great care and in a special sequence, rather like a priest putting on his vestments. And when you have finished you don't sit down again until it's all over.

Socks and shoes go on first, then the white cotton trousers, immaculately pressed. The T-shirt follows and with a loud ripping noise Marine-Corps-issue masking tape is torn off and wound around the waist to bind the trousers and undershirt together. More tape is used to attach the back of the trouser bottoms to the welts of the shoes.

The blue blouse follows, and lint particles are removed from its wrinkleless surface by tape wound around the hand. Velcro now binds the distinctive high marine collar, the descendant of the tall leather stock that gave the marines their nickname — "leatherneck." The gouging metal hooks of old have disappeared without lament.

The hat, or "cover" in Marinese, is placed on the head at the approved angle, and the human being inside all of this is ready for the show. He must, however, remain in a vertical position for the duration. Sitting down would produce fatal crease marks in the white cotton trousers, and that would never do.

As each item goes on, the sartorial uniqueness of the barracks emerges. The hat, the "barracks cover," has its crown pitched at a flatter angle to its peak than is normal in the corps at large. The white trousers are worn nowhere else. The shoes have special metal cleats on heel and toe to make a crisp, quintessentially military sound on asphalt. There is a special blue overcoat for winter events. The officers at 8th and I wear leather Sam Brownes, unique in the corps.

The rifle is the old M-1 Garand of World War II and Korea fame, its wooden stock sanded and repeatedly oiled until it is as glossy as the flanks of a thoroughbred mare. The butt plate is metal, and the rifle with bayonet weighs thirteen and a half pounds, several pounds heavier than the marines' standard M-16 rifle.

What isn't worn is as important as what is. Marines who normally wear glasses

Following pages
Preparation for the Friday evening parade at Marine Barracks, a popular summer attraction in the capital
Lieutenant Colonel Kevin M. Kennedy, executive officer, Marine Barracks
Master Gunnery Sergeant Gene G. Grafenstein, operations chief, Marine Barracks

are issued contact lenses for parades. The hard version is provided by Uncle Sam, but if a marine prefers soft lenses he has to dip into his own pocket.

After dressing, there are three squad bay inspections and a company formation, when the marines are briefed about their audience, especially about the VIPs who will be present. After that, they march out to Ninth Street for a warm up and finally move quietly into the darkened arcade to await their cue.

"There is a special feeling on Fridays," says a lance corporal with thirty-four parades under his bleached white belt. "You march out and you stop. There are five thousand people watching you. You have to concentrate and keep in time with everyone else. There are 209 marines out there. You keep a beat in your head. You order arms, and there's one butt bang, and you feel tremendous. The crowd usually reacts to that, especially the people in the peanut gallery on the bleachers at the south end. They're usually great. Once this year they even sang the national anthem."

What about that curious style of marching, the clockwork toy-soldier effect of a couple of hundred men moving as if they were being guided by an unseen hand pressing a button on an electric motor? "We go through a ceremonial drill school when we first come here, and they teach us the 'slide and glide.' The idea is to march without bouncing up and down."

Is it difficult?

"Oh, no—you just walk like a girl."

Inside the barracks the bleachers are filling up. Outside there is a big summer crowd, waiting to get in. Among them, in civilian clothes, move security men, listening, watching. Over on Ninth Street, where senators and congressmen now live in a neighborhood that has undergone intense gentrification in recent years, the Silent Drill Platoon is warming up. A civilian, showing all the signs of being a marine "groupie," watches with a critical eye.

The platoon is practicing the routine in which the marines spin their rifles with fixed bayonets and march through each other's ranks. It looks highly dangerous, but there are no wounded, walking or otherwise, when they take a break for iced water in a vat on the sidewalk.

The Silent Drill Platoon is commanded by a captain and a staff sergeant. The men who perform are infantry "grunts," between nineteen and twenty years old, 5′ 10″ to 6′ 3″ in height, and all must have White House security clearance. There is endless practice on the parade ground and in front of long metal mirrors in the underground parking of the Bachelor Enlisted Quarters alongside the barracks.

The big push comes when the platoon heads south in the spring and the choreography for the coming season is prepared by the squad leaders, who use graph paper (one square represents a thirty-inch step) for each movement. Bayonets are used all the time so the marines become accustomed to their weight and potential lethalness. "Sure, people get cut from time to time," says the captain commanding the platoon. "But they heal up pretty quickly. A bigger problem is getting a new bayonet if one is broken."

The routines for the coming parade season are presented to the commanding officer of the barracks for approval. The rule of thumb is "difficult but doable," and the ten-minute display, with its twirling rifles, intricate marching, and mock inspection, where rifles are tossed high into the air and caught with nonchalant ease—all done without verbal commands—is a highlight of the marines' ceremonial repertoire.

Last-minute preparations are going on over the wall in the barracks. The horticulturist, a full-time female civilian, has ensured that the Kentucky bluegrass on the parade ground has had its regulation watering of a minimum of one inch that week. (The watering takes place on Saturdays, Sundays, and Tuesdays. She also keeps a close watch on the stately oak trees and the hemlock firs that ring the parade ground.)

The grass has had its "ceremonial cut"—on the diagonal to make the parade

Rife company rehearses for the evening parade
Following pages
Barracks scenes (clockwise from top left): the gunny; take five; Fix Bayonets; silent drill
Silent Drill Platoon in "charlies."
Members of the platoon perform intricate drill movements with fixed bayonets and without any verbal commands
Lowering the colors: Center Walk, Marine Barracks

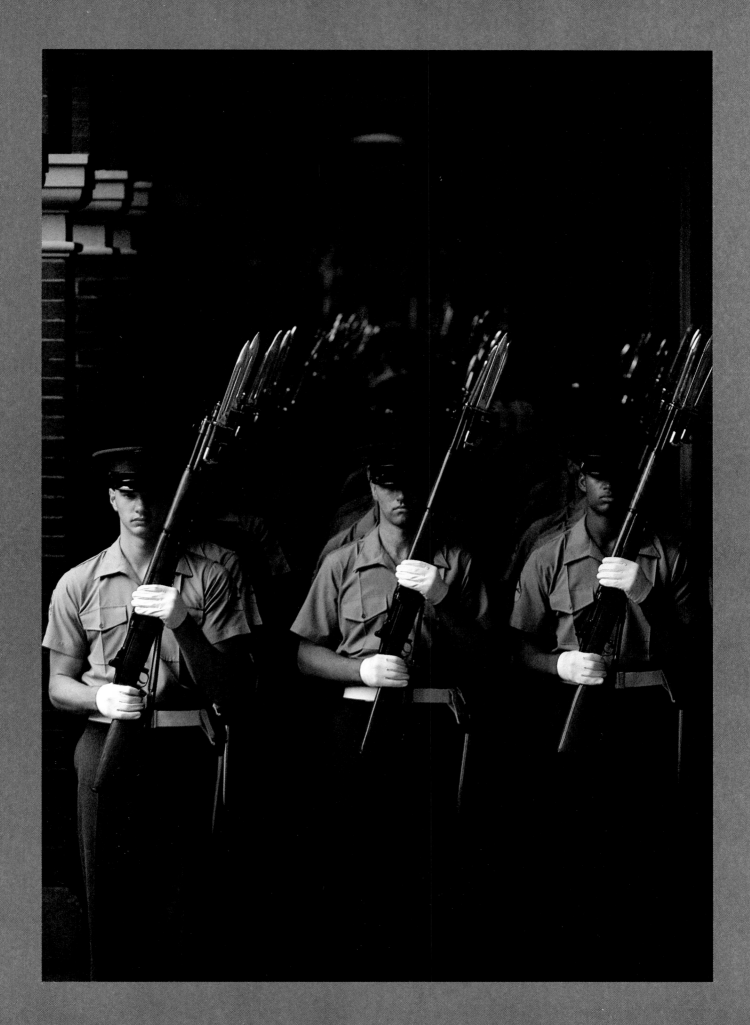

ground look longer and wider to the spectators in the stands—and is no more than the regulation three inches in height. Bald spots have been treated with a water-based blue-green paint.

The Color Guard is taking the national flag and the Marine Corps battle color out of their cases and doing last-minute checks on their uniforms. There are nineteen men in the section, but the actual Color Guard for each ceremonial event consists of four marines: the bearers of the two colors in the center, each flanked by a rifleman.

The man in charge has the sonorous title, "color sergeant of the United States Marine Corps." Only three other men share the designation "of the U.S. Marine Corps": the commandant, the assistant commandant, and the sergeant major of the Marine Corps, and it is the senior billet for sergeants in the marines.

Like the U.S. Marine Band, the Drum and Bugle Corps, and the Silent Drill Platoon, the Color Guard is part of the Marine Corps' public persona and travels widely doing its thing at events ranging from White House state dinners to "shots" like helping train a church group called the "Community of Jesus Marching Band" in Cape Cod. All the members of the guard are from combat arms background. They have to be between 6′3″ and 6′5″ in height and are what the color sergeant (himself 6′5″, weighing in at 220 pounds) calls "generic body types," i.e.—big.

Carrying a thirty-five-pound flag in a high wind is not as simple as it might sound. The Marine Corps, with typical machismo, insists that the color bearers use only one arm, unlike the other services, who permit both arms to be used. One of the tricks is to rotate the staff so that the flapping flag does not blind the bearer. If the flag does envelop its carrier, the other members of the guard give guidance by applying shoulder pressure and whispering commands.

Also backstage another participant is preparing himself or, more accurately, having himself prepared. Lance Corporal Chesty VIII is a long way from being the standard minimum height for a barracks marine, but what he lacks in stature he makes up in girth. An English pedigree bulldog named after General Lewis "Chesty" Puller, one of the Marine Corps' most colorful heroes, Chesty stands patiently while his blue blouse is put on and fastened with a Velcro tape beneath his sturdy stomach. (For rehearsals, like all the other marines, he wears the "Charlie" uniform.)

Chesty is the Marine Corps mascot. The corps' indefatigable public affairs department has a "bio" on him: "Chesty is the son of Champion Bowag's Airborne Sunnyday and Bomar's Cottontop. He is a graduate of the Canine Training Association Obedience Class for Dogs. The corps' youngest marine enlisted on February 4, 1986, at Marine Barracks."

An officer in the barracks keeps him at home, but Chesty also has an official handler, another lance corporal who looks after him during the day and takes him out for the mascot's brief moment of glory during the parade. "He's pretty lackadaisical and gets on with most people," says the handler. "During the parade he's supposed to walk out with me and sit on my left for a couple of minutes for photo opportunities. After the parade he meets the VIPs and the kids, who love him."

The previous mascot—they are all called Chesty—wasn't so lovable and occasionally tried to take his supper out of someone's leg, a trait that may have led to early retirement. And even this more benign Chesty doesn't always walk and sit when he should. But when he does he gets a cheer from the crowd. (One wonders what his namesake, were he still alive, might think of all this.)

Up in the south tower a staff sergeant who is otherwise a combat engineer is checking his lighting section. Floodlights, positioned at the center of the parade ground, are operated by the staff sergeant himself with a dimmer board. Spots are handled by his staff in both towers. Everyone is wired for sound and connected with a central control down on the ground.

Earlier in the day, the staff sergeant had gone through the parade sequence with his teams in the south and north towers. He had kept up a constant patter, encouraging

Marine Corps
battle colors and
Color Guard

and sometimes chiding as the rehearsal unrolled: "North tower stand by. Next shot will be the sergeant major at the guidons, reaaady . . . SHOT. After the report sequence the next shot will be—got to give 'em a good one tonight—a nice smooooooth spot. Stand by, reaaady . . . SPOT . . . cut! Here comes the mascot. Let's hope he walks today. Last time he sat down and wouldn't move. Pissed me off."

Now the crews, perched thirty feet off the ground, wait in the gathering gloom. In addition to operating the lights the crews have to keep their eyes peeled for airborne equipment and for falling marines. Once or twice during the parade season, a marine collapses and has to be carried off.

Over in the "sound room" a sergeant takes out a script and prepares to read along with a tape of his own voice like a prompter in the theater. He is the "voice of the barracks," handpicked as the official announcer by the commandant and the commanding officer of 8th and I. If the tape of his prerecorded commentary breaks during the parade the sound man will switch over to a live broadcast, and the sergeant reckons he should not miss more than a word.

Every show has its stage director, and the marines are no exception. Down behind the bleachers is a master gunnery sergeant wearing a headset and talking softly into his microphone. He is the pivotal figure in the drama about to unfold. The essential trick of the trade, he says, is to anticipate disaster.

To that end this low-profile master of ceremonies has, hiding in the arcade, additional troops to pick up fallen equipment or, if necessary, to replace someone in trouble. If a platoon sergeant notices that a marine is feeling ill he will tip off the "extras" by putting one hand behind his back, an unmistakable signal since there is no such drill movement in the Marine Corps.

The main problems are bayonets that refuse to lock into place, a broken rifle, a hat that goes askew or is about to fall off, a man beginning to sway. "Most of the time the public doesn't know what is happening," says the master gunnery sergeant, "though there will always be a few people who will spot it.

"I take all this very seriously," he continues. "It's not just a parade, it's a show, and there are a lot of theatrics involved. And we get some good feedback after the parade. Of course, they're not going to walk up to me and say your parade stank. But it's very emotional. I've heard them say it makes them really feel like an American. I've seen people leave here in tears."

IWO JIMA MEMORIAL, NOVEMBER 10

A cold hard rain is sluicing down over the flag raisers, reducing their giant dimensions but enhancing their heroic quality. The flag on the world's largest bronze statue is hopelessly wrapped around its staff. The seats put out for honored guests, this 212th birthday of the United States Marine Corps, are half empty.

Clusters of large umbrellas in marine scarlet and gold protect those who came. There is a handful of spectators on the muddy bank that rises up behind the seats: an old couple under a green blanket, some young women, a father taking a picture of his marine son, with a plastic cover over his camera, and a jolly family who doesn't seem to mind a midmorning drenching.

A call to the 8th and I Barracks public affairs office earlier had elicited a cheery "The parade will be held, come rain or shine." Never was a truer word spoken. Above the lush green of tree and turf that cradles this most dramatic of war memorials, gray clouds chase each other across a gray sky. As the band marches out, the rain lashes down more fiercely, water cascading off the instruments but not, at least to a layman's ear, affecting the sound.

The ceremony is short, but it is conducted as if it were a balmy summer's day. The U.S. Marine Band and the Drum and Bugle Corps do their stuff on the soggy grass, the riflemen march and drill, colors are presented, there is an invocation, speeches are given by the preceding commandant (bareheaded, attired in civilian suit and sopping rain-

NCO's sword detail
Following pages
Evening parade:
final instructions
Silent Drill Platoon
at Iwo Jima Memorial
Colonel Harvey
C. Barnum, Jr., Medal
of Honor winner,
and guests at
the evening parade

coat) and by his uniformed successor, a wreath is laid, a final prayer is said, and then all march off.

As the band passes the stand for the last time and the rifle companies zigzag around the side of the memorial and disappear from sight, there is a feeling of desolation, perhaps akin to the emotional exhaustion and depression that men experience after winning an epic battle. The gusting rain and sharpening chill on this Marine Corps birthday has brought participants and spectators closer to the reality of war, mortality, and haphazard fate. Iwo Jima, too, was cold, wet, and gray for much of the time during those terrible thirty-six days in early 1945.

Uncommon valor was indeed a common virtue among the marines during that battle, but a final glance back at the memorial, now almost completely obscured by the rain, reminds us that, of the six men who raised the flag on Mount Surabachi, three died before the battle was over, two succumbed to alcoholism back home, and only one completed the return journey to normal life.

The Royal Marine Connection, England

We share a common heritage with the United States Marines," says the Royal Marine general. "But it's not just history. There's something different about being a soldier of the sea, no matter where you come from."

The connection between the United States Marines and its British counterpart, the Royal Marines, goes back to the birth of the corps itself. The Second Continental Congress, sitting in Philadelphia, created the American marines in 1775 to fight the British at sea and modeled them on the Royal Marines. U.S. and British marines clashed again in the War of 1812, but thereafter they have fought on the same side. There is an exchange program between the two units, involving a handful of officers and staff NCOs and regular joint exercises. Each side sends its best men in the exchange, and there is considerable rivalry, albeit friendly, during the war games. Apart from history and the continuing living connection, what seems to bind them even more closely is the sense that they are both special yet vulnerable in their own societies.

"They look huge to us. We're a mere seven thousand and they're two hundred thousand," says another Royal Marine officer. "But I think we both sometimes feel threatened by our respective service rivals and defense bureaucracies who tend to see all marines as an anachronism."

Rattling around in their vast red brick Victorian barracks at Eastney on England's south coast, the Royal Marines do indeed look small. Like all Britain's armed forces, they have shrunk in size as imperial power and purse contracted. In many respects, they cannot be properly compared with the U.S. Marine Corps. Apart from size, the Royal Marines have no ships, fighter aircraft, tanks, or artillery. "It's sad," commented a U.S. Marine officer on a joint exercise in Norway. "An amphibious force without its own ships."

In some ways, the Royal Marines are closer to the U.S. Marines' reconnaissance units. Recruit training for the Royal Marines is three times as long as it is for the average American marine and includes infantry training and such specialized warfare skills as rock climbing, small-boat training, and hand-to-hand combat. Officers do a tough one-year course and then spend a further year on probation.

Three young United States Marine captains, on duty in London, have come down for the day to see their British comrades and have their picture taken. In dress uniform, the Americans in blue and the British in black with white shirts, looking a little like London police inspectors, they are not easily distinguishable. Contemporary military history, however, sets them apart. The Royal Marine officers have campaign medals: two of them fought in the Falklands War and the third has a Northern Ireland

Commandant's change of command ceremony, with the commandant's house in the background, at Marine Barracks

ribbon. The Americans, too young to have been in Vietnam, have as yet undecorated chests.

The splendor of Victorian England lives on at Eastney, although the Royal Marines will not be enjoying it much longer, since they are gradually moving out. A gun emplacement behind massive walls and overlooking the sea has been turned into the commanding general's garden. There is the Royal Marines' museum, formerly the officers' mess; beautifully organized and full of interesting artifacts, it includes a wax model of a U.S. Marine in a World War I uniform with gas mask and Springfield rifle.

The young officers take a drink in the general's dining room, whose gleaming mahogany table, crystal, and silver candlesticks make an elegant backdrop for the occasion. A mess corporal, who looks after the general's uniform, casts a critical eye on one of the Royal Marine lieutenant's medals and notices that the edges haven't been cleaned. "Look at that," he says, *sotto voce*, "lazy bugger." Then he gives the U.S. Marines the once over. "I'd mug them for those Corfam shoes," he says wistfully.

"I have the greatest admiration for the U.S. Marines," the general says over a sherry. "They put in a very creditable performance in Norway last winter although they aren't as used to the snow as we are. But they had a rough period with all kinds of disciplinary and morale problems in the early seventies. We did some exercises with them in the Mediterranean, and I remember a black NCO, an old-timer, saying to me: "They talk of the old corps, they talk of the new corps, but dis is shit!""

A British military correspondent who had spent time with both units had this to say: "The U.S. Marines are very un-American in some ways. They are ultraneat and tidy, clean and disciplined." He was interested in the differences in recruit training. Boot camp at Parris Island, he thought, was more "mentally savage" than the Royal Marines' basic training in which, he said, the method was to tighten the screw gradually and to build up toughness. With the British there was less mental abuse, but the training was harder physically, and cursing and occasional physical punishment were accepted. Like all British military observers, he was in awe of the amount of military hardware at the U.S. Marines' disposal.

A view from the other side comes from a "recon" marine who served with the British in the mid-seventies.

"I like the way they operate," he says. "They expect you to become a Royal Marine. It was very rugged. You have to pass the commando course and prove yourself. Their NCOs are some of the best in the world, although the officers are more laid back. The troops responded well to a Yank in command. I really had a good time."

The U.S. Marines have similar fraternal ties with the Dutch Marines through an exchange program of officers and staff NCOs. There are also close connections with the Philippine and the South Korean Marines, and during the Vietnam War the relationship with the South Vietnam Marines was important. But the links with the British are the tightest not only in a technical sense but also in what each represents in its own society and culture. The word "marine" in the United States and Britain, evokes history, military machismo, aggressiveness, and derring-do. It is no accident that the Royal Marines have appropriated the sexy term "commando" for their units (a word that was first coined by the Boer guerrillas in the Anglo-Boer War in South Africa), nor that they led the British assault on the Falklands in 1982.

But this also means a high profile and a long fall when things go wrong. While the U.S. Marine Corps has to live with its Ollie Norths and Moscow security guard scandals, the Royal Marines have to live with—or rather without—their royal neophytes. Prince Edward, Queen Elizabeth's youngest son, decided to leave the Royal Marines after completing only a third of his officer training. He quit, according to Royal Marine officers, not because he lacked the necessary physical and mental abilities but probably because his royal position—he was guarded night and day by private detectives—cut him off from his comrades. In short, he was a lonely young man, and lonely young men do not usually make good marines on either side of the Atlantic.

Brother officers:
U.S. Marines
and Royal Marines
at Eastney Barracks,
England

Marine Security Guard, Paris

For anyone who has traveled abroad and dropped into a U.S. embassy or consulate, a United States marine in dress blues directing the flow of visitors through the main entrance is a common sight.

The United States embassy in Paris is also what you might expect: an elegant, high-ceilinged affair with curving staircases and somber portraits on the walls, set back from the tree-lined Champs-Elysées. Less expected, however, are the Delta metal barriers that, at the push of a button, rise up out of the ground and stop dead any approaching vehicle except a tank; the bulletproof booth in the embassy's entrance; and the deadly array of weapons, including Remington 12-gauge shotguns, tear gas grenades, Magnum pistols, Uzi submachine guns, and .38 revolvers in the Marine Security Guard's armory inside the building.

Master Gunnery Sergeant Richard Carlisle is a veteran of embassy guard duty, that peculiarly American institution that employs servicemen to protect U.S. diplomatic missions around the world. (No other nation guards its embassies in this way.) He has served in Copenhagen, New Delhi, Tokyo, and Paris. He is expecting a new—and final—assignment soon.

"In the old days," says Carlisle, who still wears real leather shoes, "defenses were the last thing they thought of. We used to be the glory detail, standing around at parade rest in our dress blues and smiling at everybody. Most of the time we wouldn't even be armed."

But the growth of terrorism in the 1970s and in particular the 1983 suicide car bombing of the U.S. embassy in Beirut changed all that. Embassies' physical defenses have been greatly strengthened; military attachés, intelligence officers, and other high-risk personnel now take special precautions, and the marine guards have become highly tactical.

In Quantico, Virginia, where the marines are trained for embassy duty, Colonel Sean Del Grosso, their commanding officer, points to the anomalies inherent in the task.

"Diplomacy is an open, liberal process," he says. "But we're in the security business—combat diplomacy you might call it, and it's difficult and dangerous. In the decade since 1977, we have had 533 security incidents, eight men killed, eleven wounded, and fourteen captured. The last two marines to die in Vietnam were killed on embassy duty."

The Marine Corps began this unusual duty in 1949 after the State Department, unsatisfied with its civilian guards, requested help from the military. There are now 140 detachments, varying in size from six to thirty-six marines, stationed in 127 countries. This commitment involves some sixteen hundred marines, including the headquarters and training staff in Quantico, roughly the equivalent of a reinforced infantry battalion.

The detachments are always commanded by an NCO with a "company commander," normally a lieutenant colonel, based centrally in each continent or region. In Europe, for example, the officer lives in Frankfurt, West Germany, but is constantly on the move visiting detachments in other countries. Within each diplomatic mission the marine guard is under the operational command of the embassy security officer, usually a former policeman or military man, and the ambassador.

For the NCO in charge of the detachment it is a unique job because it is the only place in the Marine Corps where a noncommissioned officer has his own command.

"Most of us love the job," says Carlisle, sitting in his office in the Paris embassy. "In my last job in motor transport at Camp Pendleton, California, I had a lieutenant colonel, major, captain, and pregnant woman marine over me, and I was miserable. But

there's a tremendous amount of after-hours work in this duty because you are responsible for your men twenty-four hours a day. That means you've got to be really close to them. It's sink or swim."

The Paris embassy has the largest marine detachment in the world—thirty-six all told. The embassy is not easy to guard because it consists of five separate buildings, including the ambassador's sumptuous residence on the Rue du Faubourg St. Honoré.

"Our basic mission," says Carlisle, "is to protect people and property inside these buildings. Security outside the embassy is the responsibility of the host country, as it is in all parts of the world. We check classified areas after hours and issue violations if necessary. A marine, armed with a shotgun, will occasionally check the garbage as it is taken out."

Bomb threats were coming in at the rate of about two a month, and Carlisle stopped his men from running together in a squad; they now train in pairs. The marines also keep changing their route between the embassy and the marine house, which are about a mile apart. All the marines have beepers and can be called out of bed or a bar at a moment's notice. Carlisle says that in an emergency he can muster at least half his detachment within ten minutes. He sometimes practices by pushing the panic button at the embassy at 3:00 A.M.

Carlisle's men have longer hair than most marines but not long enough to excite the puritan conscience of the corps. (The price of a French haircut helps to curb the instincts of the compulsive head shaver.) All marines on embassy duty, with the exception of the staff NCOs in charge, have to be single, and in Paris they are not allowed to own cars or motorcycles or to shack up with a girlfriend.

Some bars are put off limits occasionally, and marines must move around in pairs at least; the buddy system is strongly encouraged. Moderation in drinking is advised, and Carlisle thinks one of the best ways to produce that effect is a vigorous PT program. "Who the hell wants to get ripped and then go out for a five-mile run the next morning?" he asks. "We're not here to pull liberty."

Colonel Del Grosso in Quantico briefs ambassadors and their wives on the marines' role before they take up their posts. "I suggest they visit Post One, the booth at the embassy's entrance, and ask the marine what he does there. I also recommend they go to the marine house where the detachment lives, and to let the marines go to their residence when they are not in to study the lie of the land. One day the marines may have to fight in there. Another piece of advice I give is: 'No first names—no Dick, Jane, and Harry—that kind of thing doesn't work where the rubber meets the road.'"

Carlisle and other detachment commanders around the world often play the 'what if' game to help train their men. "The marines must be both tactful and tactical," he says. "We get a lot of verbal abuse and aggravation from students in Paris, and I try to encourage the guys to take it out in the PT program. One of the 'what if' exercises has a demonstration outside the embassy. Another has three suicidal bombers inside the chancery building and one grabs the ambassador. Our response would be to find them, seal them off, and hand them over to the French police and negotiators.

"Then there is the ambassador's residence. The only time we go over there is for receptions like the Fourth of July, when we're dressed in blues. But even then I insist on us all being armed with .38 revolvers. The ambassador is our boss, and I feel funny if I'm not armed. He is our commanding officer, and we don't want anything to happen to him. The only other time we'd go there would be if the shit hit the fan. We'd get over there fast and if necessary fight our way up floor by floor and get him out. I know these marines would die defending the embassy."

The assumption these days is that no foreign country is really safe for embassy personnel, especially military attachés, intelligence officials, and the marines. There is a chilling reminder of this in the lobby of the Paris embassy, where a plaque honoring Colonel Charles Robert Ray, Assistant Army Attaché, greets the visitor. In 1982, Colonel Ray was killed by an assassin's bullet on a Paris street in broad daylight.

Del Grosso and Carlisle both say that the State Department and most ambassadors have become much more security conscious in the eighties and show a greater appreciation for the operational capabilities of their marines than they used to. This is a plus and a minus for the marines. They like the idea of action. "At the drop of a hat we can take this off"—Carlisle gestures to his civilian suit—"and put on our combat gear, grab a Remington or an Uzi, and be ready for business." But it also means a more restricted lifestyle for the young men, even in relatively safe and friendly places like Western Europe.

Over in the marine house in Paris, a French cook who has been there for sixteen years is preparing an American-style lunch for the marines. Each marine has his own room. There is a laundry, TV and pool rooms, two weight rooms, a disco (Friday is the big night), and a plaque on the wall displaying the "Marine of the Month," rather in the way hotels publicize their best employee. Marines work around the clock on a shift system, eight hours on at a time. They can mix with whomever they choose off duty, but if they meet Soviet bloc nationals they must report the fact to the detachment commander. They can spend a night out of the marine house with Carlisle's permission, but only if they have the next day off.

"I tell my marines," says Carlisle, "if you want to have a few drinks and hire a hotel room or go to your girlfriend's place, that's fine. But not in the marine house. A moral code is important; if not, there's chaos."

Embassy duty, at least on the surface, doesn't seem like much fun. Standing watch hour after hour, day after day, must be boring, and the marine house is just another barracks. But the job is prize duty in the Marine Corps, both for the enlisted men and the staff NCOs, all of whom have to volunteer and are carefully selected and trained at Quantico. A tour usually lasts thirty months, half in a "soft" post, like a Western European country, and the remainder in a hardship post, such as a remote Third World capital or behind the iron curtain.

The NCOs like the job because it gives them freedom and command. For once in their careers they will not have officers breathing down their necks. Embassy duty ranks with the other high-profile, high-risk billets for NCOs: recruiting and the drill field. The difference is that, unlike the other two jobs, it can also be dangerous. "You can get hurt on this duty," says Colonel Del Grosso.

Detachment commanders and their deputies are accompanied by their wives, who receive a one-week course at Quantico. Most of the wives adapt to a foreign environment, but there are occasional "cultural casualties." "Even the best marines are no good," Del Grosso says, "if their chief of staff decides to pack up and leave."

The reason why the young marines like it is because they are young marines. Youthfulness absorbs the tedium of watch standing because it is offset by the novelty of travel and living abroad, by the VIPs and other new people they meet, and by the sense of elitism that goes with the job. As marines, they enjoy the camaraderie of a small unit, the public platform that allows them to strut their stuff, and the esteem and enhanced chances of promotion that are inherent in having done embassy duty. "It's a jewel in the career crown of an enlisted man," says Del Grosso.

None of this seems to have been disturbed by the Moscow embassy marine guard scandal in 1987, although the collapse of discipline there and the subsequent indictments of marines on charges of espionage and fraternization were a trauma of immense proportions for the corps and for many past and present marines.

Fifteen thousand marines had served all around the world over a forty-year period when the scandal broke. The record, on the whole, was good to excellent with some minor lapses redeemed by steady service and heroic actions in extremely difficult

Following page
Master Gunnery Sergeant Richard W. Carlisle with his Marine Security Guard detachment in the courtyard of the U.S. ambassador's residence on the Rue du Faubourg St. Honoré, Paris

places and situations. Marine guards have fought off storming mobs, put out fires, and saved people from drowning.

But with a self-propelled high-profile organization like the Marine Corps, tarnish is more easily detected than glitter by the media and the public. A sweeping investigation into the troubled Moscow embassy led to revelations that marine detachments in other missions also had disciplinary problems.

Of the marines in the eye of the "sex-for-secrets" storm, only one, Sergeant Clayton J. Lonetree, was eventually convicted. He received a sentence of thirty years in prison—later reduced to twenty-five—for espionage. Charges against other Marine Security Guards were dropped, but some were demoted or discharged from the corps for fraternization and other lesser offenses. Charges that the marines had let Soviet intelligence officers roam around secure sections of the embassy—the most damaging accusation of all—were dropped because of lack of evidence. However, an agonizing reappraisal by the Marine Corps and State Department was set in motion.

"It was a double failure of leadership," explained a senior marine officer in Washington. "The embassy security officer failed and so did our detachment commander." Master Gunnery Sergeant Carlisle puts the bulk of the blame on the detachment commander and his deputy. "Where were those guys?" he asks. "They walked away from the job."

While the Marine Corps accepted at least part of the blame and prosecuted the perpetrators, it did not punish the NCOs in charge of the detachments for their failure of leadership. It was clear that the ambassador as commander-in-chief of the Moscow embassy was also culpable and was later held responsible for the misconduct of marines there by a presidential panel appointed to investigate the affair.

"This thing only works when three things happen," says Colonel Del Grosso. "The ambassador has to be security conscious, there has to be a good State Department security officer, and we have to have the right kind of detachment commander."

In the aftermath of the Moscow scandal, the length of the duty in such sensitive posts as the Soviet Union has been reduced and the selection process of marines made even more stringent. With one problem receding, another one has arisen. The Pentagon, in its drive to expand the role of women in the armed services, has ordered the Marine Corps, much against its will, to post women marines overseas as security guards. A pilot program was tried by the corps in 1979–80, but it did not lead to women doing the duty. The corps' view is that embassy guard duty is potentially so dangerous that it requires "combat-ready marines drawn principally from the combat-arms occupational fields." Those categories are not open to women. However, visitors to U.S. missions abroad may soon be greeted by a woman marine in blues, carrying a sidearm, baton, and handcuffs, in that bulletproof glass cubicle.

Summing up, Colonel Del Grosso believes that on embassy duty, 89 percent of the infractions by marines come down to "wine and women." Master Gunnery Sergeant Carlisle disagrees. "The biggest problem," he says, "is not booze and women. It is remaining a marine and remembering what that means. One of the worst things that can happen on this duty is that a marine 'goes State'—that is, becomes a civilian."
[*Postscript.* In early 1988, Carlisle received his new assignment: detachment commander in Moscow.]

Belleau Wood, France

They tried new tactics to get the bayonets into the Bois de Belleau. Platoons—very lean platoons now—formed in small combat groups, deployed in the wheat, and set out toward the gloomy wood. . . . The shells ripped overhead, and the wood was full of leaping flame. . . . The fire from its edge died down. It was late afternoon; the sun was low enough to shine under the edge of your helmet. The men went forward at a walk, their shoulders hunched over, their bodies inclined, their eyes on the edge of the wood, where shrapnel was raising a hell of a dust. Some of them had been this way before; their faces were set bleakly. Others were replacements, a month or so from Quantico; they were terribly anxious to do the right thing, and they watched zealously the sergeants and the corporals and the lieutenants who led the way with canes. |John W. Thomason, *Fix Bayonets!*

It is Memorial Day, an American holiday in a peaceful corner of a foreign land. The cemetery is unusual: two graceful arcs of white crosses and stars of David flank a Romanesque chapel with a tall tower. In front is a lawn that doubles as a parade ground for such occasions as this. It is a peerless day of warm spring sunshine, flowering roses, rhododendrons, and cherries, and dancing butterflies. The sweet scent of lilac blossom is everywhere.

Visitors and guests are taking their places for the annual ceremony that celebrates the marines' greatest exploit in Europe. It happened almost seventy years ago, but the brooding wood of Belleau, with its wounded trees, buried bric-a-brac of war, and ghosts of Americans and Germans who fought to the death in its shadows, sits above the cemetery looking much as it did in the hot and violent summer of 1918.

The Fourth Marine Brigade, recently arrived in France, was thrown into the crumbling line in the Marne Valley as the Germans launched their last great offensive of the war. The marines fought on many fronts, alongside their army comrades in the Second Division with its famous Indian head insignia and commanded by Major General John A. Lejeune, the first time an army division was commanded by a marine. But the epic struggle for the strategic heights of Belleau Wood, a twenty-acre plateau standing above the rolling wheat fields of this lush part of France, remained ingrained in the military memories of their allies, the French, and their enemies, the Germans, alike.

The battle raged for three weeks as the marines and the army infantry slowly dislodged the entrenched Germans and captured the wood. More than two thousand Americans lie buried in the cemetery; fourteen thousand Germans are interred in a plot of land surrounded by plane trees a rifle shot away, and many hundreds more probably lie under the trees in the wood above, buried in the sandy soil.

After the battle the French commander of the Sixth Army officially renamed the wood the Bois de la Brigade de Marine in honor of the United States Marines who had fought, died, and conquered. General Lejeune, writing later about the battle, called the wood "holy ground." The Germans also paid tribute. They gave the marines a new name: *teufelhunden* ("devil-dogs").

A marine honor guard, twenty-five men strong, from the embassy in Paris is formed up on one side of the lawn. On the other side are detachments of French infantry and marines, accompanied by a band. The dignitaries, including the French *préfet*, the American ambassador, a marine general, the French general commanding the region, and Belleau's mayor, take their seats in front of the chapel.

A hole in the chapel wall is a reminder of another war. It was made by a German antitank gun firing at French tanks in the blitzkrieg through France in 1940. But the rest of the cemetery is immaculate, the responsibility of Arthur Martin, the superintendent and a former soldier himself. (The night before the parade he had been scrubbing lichen off the chapel walls with bleach.)

Tiny American and French flags flutter in front of the headstones. Birds swoop and sing in the woods above and dazzling shards of sunlight rebound off the band's instruments. Local people in their Sunday best file into the seats behind the VIPs. There are many *anciens combatants*, small grizzled men in berets with clusters of medals on their chests. There are some Americans, too. One, whose son is in the marines in Okinawa, Japan, expresses surprise at the number of marines on parade. "I didn't know the marines were in Europe," he says.

The marines, in dress blues, look older and larger than their French counterparts. Earlier, one of them, in the rear rank, had passed out, falling backward and bouncing lightly on the springy turf like a felled tree. It transpires that he has a history of collapsing but had omitted to tell anyone. He recovers quickly but doesn't rejoin the parade.

The master gunnery sergeant in charge of the detachment moves out in front of his men. "Listen," he says, "this is a very special, very historic place for us. I've always wanted to come here. Be proud and shine today. I want you guys to strut. Remember you're United States Marines!"

The band strikes up and the parade begins. The marines fire three volleys, there is a drum roll from the tower of the chapel, and floral wreaths are laid—splashes of color against the green grass and the gray stones. The speeches recall the old friendship, in war and in peace, between the United States and France. The marine general points out that in the battle of Yorktown, which ended America's War of Independence, French casualties were three times as great as those sustained by Washington's American forces.

The American ambassador springs a surprise by telling his audience that his father fought at Belleau Wood in the U.S. Army and wrote letters to his mother about the carnage. This lady, ninety-one years old and frail but alert, stands at his side as he speaks. The mayor of Belleau, who has visited Quantico as a guest of the Marine Corps, recalls that two great conflicts have rolled over these peaceful fields. He ends as simply as he began: "Thanks to the young soldiers who lie here with us. Thanks to their comrades in combat. Thanks to their families. Thanks to the American nation."

After the "Star-Spangled Banner" and the "Marseillaise" have been played the ceremony moves into the woods. To the steady beat of a snare drum, the troops march up a small path to a road shaded by elm, silver birch, pine, and beech trees. Some of the older trees still bear the scars of the battle. The trees are "sacred"—that is, no one is allowed to cut them down without permission. Hunting is not allowed either, and the wood has become a refuge for deer and wild boar. Leaves and moss disguise old trenches but you can recognize them by the gentle indentation and the way your feet sink in.

In the center of the woods, the colors are presented in front of the marine memorial, a stark sculpture in bronze of a marine infantryman naked to the waist. German and French cannon from the battle line the roadside. There is a German howitzer with the kaiser's royal crest and the date 1916 engraved on the breech. There is also a large mortar base plate and several French 75mm cannon. One of the "seventy-fives," the workhorse of the French artillery, has a split barrel and looks like an elephant's mouth open in a toothless grin. Champagne is served in a tent and crates of beer have arrived for the troops. Frenchmen in khaki and Americans in blue mingle, some conversing, others looking a little bewildered.

Forever American soil, donated by a grateful ally, the wood is soon empty again, alone with its scarred trees, rusting guns, and its sleeping warriors.

Good German troops, with every device of engineering skill, and all their cunning gained in war, poured into the wood. Battalions of Marines threw themselves against it. Day and night for nearly a month men fought in its corpse-choked thickets, killing with bayonet and bomb and machine gun. It was gassed and shelled and shot into the semblance of nothing earthly. The great trees were all down; the leaves blasted off, or hung sere and blackened. It was pockmarked with shell craters and shallow dugouts and hasty trenches. It was strewn with all the debris of war, Mauser rifles and Springfields, helmets, German and American, unexploded grenades, letters, knapsacks, packs, blankets, boots; a year later, it is said, they were still finding unburied dead in the depths of it. Finally, it was taken, by inches. John W. Thomason, *Fix Bayonets!*

Memorial Day images:
The alliance;
Following pages
"**T**he Star Spangled Banner" and the "Marseillaise";
Bois de la Brigade de Marine;
A toast and a handshake

LESTER WILLIAM MARCH
PVT. 6 REGT. U.S.M.C. 2 DIV.
COLORADO JUNE 8, 1918

The Navy Cross is the navy and Marine Corps' highest award for valor in combat after the Congressional Medal of Honor. It was originally created by an act of Congress in 1919 as the third highest navy decoration, the Congressional Medal of Honor and the Distinguished Service Medal taking precedence. The award was designed for heroism in combat and other acts of gallantry. Enlisted personnel who won it were granted a two-dollar monthly gratuity. In 1942 another act of Congress upgraded the decoration to its present position and limited it to acts of heroism on the battlefield. The cross is made of bronze and shows a caravel on its obverse; the reverse bears crossed anchors and the letters USN. The ribbon is appropriate and commendably simple: navy blue with a narrow white center stripe. The marines on the following pages won Navy Crosses in World War II, Korea, and Vietnam.

George Hunt

George Hunt is in his studio working on the production of a book about Jupiter Island, which is linked by bridges to Florida's Atlantic coast. He spends part of the year there and the rest in Maine or Mexico. He has the slow movements and speech of a big man (6′3″). Evidence of his interests surround him. There is an old Remington upright typewriter and an Adler portable. "I don't like electric typewriters," he says, "because you need electricity to work them." There are bound copies of *Life* magazine on a bookshelf and a plaque of his last editorial before handing over the managing editorship in 1968, having presided over the magazine during eight of its greatest years. There is also a picture of the fifty-seven-foot ketch *Baraka,* which he once owned and crossed the Atlantic in after retiring from the magazine but not from life itself.

"I joined the Marine Corps because I had a very low draft number," George Hunt begins, "and I didn't want to be drafted. I thought about the navy, but I'd heard about the marines, so I went down to 90 Church Street in lower Manhattan—that's how it happened. This was in July 1941, before Pearl Harbor, and I was an office boy at Time, Inc. I was sent down to Quantico to join the officer candidates class. I arrived with a tennis racket, and some guys turned up with golf clubs. I thought it was going to be a leisurely course—that's what it sounded like from the brochure. It was obvious as soon as we got off the train that all this business about Quantico being a nice place was just a big fake. It was late afternoon, and we were quickly pushed into three ranks facing an embankment, with the station behind us. On the embankment was this gunnery sergeant staring down at us. You could see immediately what kind of man he was. He was standing absolutely upright, stiff and straight, a magnificent-looking man. He had a mass of decorations that included the Congressional Medal of Honor. One hand was stiff and in a black glove. He stood there and looked at us. This confrontation went on for about five minutes, and there was total silence. Then, in a quiet drawl, he gave an order to the sergeants on either flank down below the embankment and, boy, they marched us out of there fast."

Was the Marine Corps what he expected? "I didn't think it would be as rough as it was. In those days, we didn't know much about the military. I went to Amherst College, a haven of the liberal arts, and there was no talk about war. We had one military lecture every year on the battle of Jutland. I had no family in the Marine Corps, and

George Hunt's Navy Cross. The last time he wore it was when it was pinned on his greens at Quantico in the spring of 1945

there were no marines walking around in those days. I had seen some pictures of marine uniforms, but that didn't intrigue me much. I didn't even know that they had greens. When I saw this gunny with a wooden hand, he had on his greens.

"After Pearl Harbor we knew we would end up in the Pacific. I married Anita in April of 1942, just before we went down to New River, North Carolina, where we got a house on the beach. I had an old Studebaker, and with a couple of other guys I'd commute. We had a good time. I was made the regimental intelligence officer of the First Marines because I had worked for a news magazine. The executive officer of the regiment promptly called me Scoop."

Hunt went overseas in the First Marine Division and fought in Guadalcanal, New Britain, and Peleliu. He won the Navy Cross for taking and defending a coral hill that dominated the left flank of the beach on Peleliu and later wrote a marvelous account of the battle in his book *Coral Comes High*. In a strange irony, his house in Florida is built on a coral island. A large target, he was never hit. He was, in his words, "incredibly lucky." He also never wore dress blues or had a sword. "I didn't need one," he says.

Guadalcanal was important, he points out, for the defense of Australia and New Zealand, whose men were fighting with the British against the Germans in North Africa. "The invasion of Guadalcanal was confused at first because we went off the map eight hundred yards inland," he says. "We were just going on blind directions. I remember meeting the battalion intelligence officer, and we had this big row about where we were. I said we were on the bank of one river, and he said we were on the bank of another. I don't remember which one of us turned out to be right.

"Colonel Clifton B. Cates was our commanding officer. He'd won the Navy Cross in a famous platoon action at Belleau Wood in World War I and followed Vandegrift as commandant after World War II. Yet you didn't think of him as a field officer. A slender, tall, elegant man, he smoked a cigarette with a long holder. On Guadalcanal his khakis were impeccably starched and creased. He had a corporal named Strunk, who was his orderly, and Strunk took meticulous care of him.

"Guadalcanal was a time of patrolling, mapmaking, and being shelled. The navy went away and left us for a couple of months. We lived off chocolate bars and Japanese fish and rice rations. We could see the Japanese building up their forces, and their navy shelled us every night. Being on the receiving end of naval gunfire is quite horrifying because you hear this metallic *pong—whit,* and it comes in with such speed. Then you hear the metallic clang, and then it *smashes.* It *smashes* and explodes. It's an awful sound. We were all racked with malaria and jaundice. All the quinine went down with the ships sunk by the Japanese. But we had plenty of hair tonic.

"The marine aviators were fantastic on Guadalcanal. There were thirteen Grumman Hellcats, and they were all shot down. I think all the pilots were killed. More flew in from a stray carrier somewhere, and they were all killed. Those guys were unbelievable. Watching the dogfights, you'd see them knock down four or five Japs and come in to land with smoke coming out of their tails. One by one those remarkable pilots were killed."

Hunt left Guadalcanal on Christmas Day 1942, after five months on the island, and went to Australia along with what was left of the division. The next objective was New Britain. "In Australia," he says, "I developed a new patrolling system using three instead of two scouts. It gave you better flank coverage. I taught this technique to the regiment. We called it a scout-sniper school. By the time we hit New Britain, I had a sixty-man scout-sniper company that worked out of intelligence headquarters.

"This time," he continues, "we were under MacArthur and the army. The staff work under MacArthur was memorable; supplies came up on time and everything was beautifully organized. I remember the voyage to New Britain on board ship, sneaking along in the dark. The moon was up, and guys were around the deck singing 'For Me and My Gal.' It was a very sentimental, very beautiful occasion with the moon flickering on

the southern water and the songs, one after another. I also remember talking to the company commander of K Company, Third Battalion, First Marines, and he said: 'George, if I get killed, I want you to take over my company.' Well, he was killed. His executive officer took over the company and was wounded. Then I took over.

"My battalion commander called me in after the airstrip had been captured. We had lost contact with the Japanese. He said: 'Now look, Hunt, you go out there and find the Japanese or don't come back.' I'll never forget that. I decided that I wouldn't take any heavy weapons. I took three rifle platoons with light weapons, that's all.

"We ran into the Japanese in no uncertain terms outside a place called Agulapella. We came to a gorge, and down at its foot was a stream. The Japanese were on the other side of the stream, but we didn't know that at the time. The only way to find out was to go down with a unit and draw fire. I went down with three or four scouts, and we spread out and drew fire. No one was hurt, and we were able to spot their positions. I held a platoon back to fire rifles and BARs [Browning automatic rifles] smack across the stream. I sent another platoon around the left flank, with the third platoon behind it in support. Well, we had quite a nasty fight. Three men were seriously wounded, and one of them died on the way back to base. But we polished off about twenty Japs. We reached Agulapella only to find it deserted. The Japs had disappeared again. I radioed back to divisional HQ and was told that a battalion was moving up from the coast to meet us at Agulapella and that it was headed by Lieutenant Colonel Lewis 'Chesty' Puller. My company was ordered to join his battalion.

"Puller was a legendary figure in the Marine Corps, renowned as a tough troop leader. He said he had heard about my 'little fight.' He placed my company in the point position. We spent the first night along the river. Using the radio, I requested permission to cross the river at dawn with a patrol to explore the terrain on the other side. Puller responded immediately. 'Absolutely, Hunt, absolutely,' he said. So at dawn I took three three-man teams and crossed the river. I thought the whole patrol would drown. We had no rope but strung our rifle slings together and got across at a narrow point. Off we went down the trail.

"Puller's mission was to trap and kill General Matsuda's forces. We were shocked to find that all the footprints on this trail—hundreds of them—were facing us. The Japs had already gone through Agulapella, and they were now well to the west. We captured a couple of stray Japanese soldiers; they were so starved they could hardly move anyway. We were now out of radio contact with Puller's headquarters. I couldn't get his permission to continue the patrol, but I thought that I should finish the job so that the whole battalion wouldn't have to do it. Assuming that the colonel would approve, we pushed on. Three days later we reached the coast. Not a Jap there or along the way. I sent a runner back to Puller with a careful message describing what had happened and requesting an air drop of rations.

"After two days or so, a runner came back with a message from Puller. It said: 'Place yourself under arrest for disobedience of orders and return immediately.' So I placed myself under arrest by turning over the patrol to my sergeant, and we retraced our footsteps. About three quarters of the way back, there was Puller, athwart the jungle trail, glowering. He read me off from stem to stern. Then he put me under the charge of a lieutenant with a drawn pistol and confined me in a tent. Puller proceeded to take his entire battalion with its heavy weapons all the way down to the coast, over exactly the same ground that my eleven-man patrol had covered. Still no Japanese.

"After the campaign was over, and we had returned to our positions around the airfield, my battalion commander told me that I had raised a hell of a stink. I said: 'Colonel, you told me not to come back alive if I didn't find these Japanese, and the only time I found them was when they were shooting at me.' Colonel Puller had meanwhile filed court-martial charges against me, and they went up to the commanding general of the First Division, Major General Rupertus. My regimental commander, Colonel Whaling, came to my defense and interceded with the general, who summoned me to his tent.

He had a double tent with a nice bar and all kinds of booze. He offered me a scotch; it tasted awful good. And he said: 'Well, I know all about this, Hunt. I'm going to drop the whole thing, but I just wanted to give you a bit of advice. Hereafter, don't use so much initiative.' I said: 'Very well, General,' and left. General Matsuda and about three divisions of Japanese escaped from the island.

Hunt's next island was Peleliu and, by an irony of fate, Puller became his regimental commander, taking over the First Marines from Whaling. There appeared to be a good strategic reason for taking Peleliu, since it was on the flank of Mindanao in the Philippines and had an airfield. But, Hunt says, MacArthur changed his plan for the invasion of the Philippines and went in at Leyte Gulf.

"So when it was decided that Peleliu would be hit, it was in the wake of the war. The island was never used for the assault on the Philippines. But I heard that the admiral responsible said, 'Let the marines take it. Why call it off? It will be a bit of an exercise.' Our division commander, Rupertus, didn't want to call it off either. I understand that he refused to have the army join in with our First Division. Yet if we'd had two divisions we surely would have done the job quicker and with far fewer casualties.

"We had been told by a captured Japanese that the island was impregnable. Puller studied the maps and assigned every company's position. We trained day after day until we could do it blindfolded. We were prepared for this operation, believe me. Puller had given me the toughest job of taking the left flank. I think it was because he had developed a respect for my company.

"We were on the LST for twenty-two days. Finally we hit Peleliu and everything happened according to plan, except one thing. The whole second platoon, which was attacking on the right, fell into a disguised tank trap, a big pit that had been dug right across their front. It was about as deep as this room, and we hadn't seen it in the aerial photographs because it had been disguised with coconut trees and fronds. They were trapped without cover and virtually annihilated.

"The marine principle, the only principle, is that as soon as the naval gunfire and the air cover lifts, as soon as you get out of that amtrac, you run up the beach as fast and as far as you can go. You wheel to one side or the other, you charge ahead.

"On Peleliu, my first platoon did just that, dropping phosphorous grenades down the vents of the pillboxes, covering the embrasures with the Browning machine guns. The Japanese had come down through the gap left by the second platoon so I threw the third platoon in there. We took the point that enfiladed the entire regimental beach. But the Japanese came around behind and surrounded us. Colonel Puller knew precisely what to do. He sent four amtracs full of grenades up to the point. One amtrac got through, the other three were hit and blew up. We defended the point for another seventy-two hours, and L Company pushed up the hill to join us. We kept going for another ten days, and then we were relieved. Meanwhile, on the right, the Fifth Regiment got involved in fighting in the caves. After the island was secure, the army came in. Our regiment had lost 70 percent of its strength. I had landed with a full-strength company, about 235 men; after the battle there were only about thirty-five of us left.

"Later, going up the coast, we used dogs—fantastic as messengers—Dobermans and one German shepherd. We put messages on their collars. The radios didn't work, nothing ever works in a fight. Some of the time even your own artillery is mashing you up; it's crazy, there's no rhyme or reason. But you just have to weather it, and keep pushing. That's what Puller used to say. 'Keep pushin', Hunt, keep pushin'.'

"Puller's brother had been killed on Guam, and he was in pain from an old thigh wound. He was a gentleman and a great leader. I had heard that his letters home were poetic, beautifully written. We got back onto the ship and went into the wardroom and stood at the table behind our chairs, waiting for Puller. He came in, and we all sat down. He looked terribly pale and haggard, as we all probably did, and he gazed down at me with those penetrating eyes. 'I'm glad to see you back, Hunt,' he said loudly so everyone could hear. It was nice."

George Hunt won the Silver Star in New Britain and got the Navy Cross in Peleliu. "These medals to a commanding officer," he says, "are for the company. Every member of my company deserved a Navy Cross. And the guys in the company were as proud of me getting the Navy Cross as I was. It's their cross as much as it is mine." He gets up and opens a small box. The medal is stained and salty looking, more impressive in its way than if it had been kept beautifully polished.

In *Coral Comes High,* Hunt tells of one night during the battle for the point when he suddenly awoke and threw himself sideways. The tree under which he had been sleeping toppled over and fell on the spot where he had been lying seconds earlier. That was his closest encounter with death throughout the war.

"Premonition can happen," he says. "It becomes more dramatic in a combat situation or in one that is going to become a combat situation. For example, the commander of the second platoon who walked into the tank trap on Peleliu knew he was going to die. I knew he was going to be killed because he knew he was going to be killed. And I think everyone knew it, and everyone tried to reassure him that he was not going to be killed, which just further convinced him that he was going to be killed.

"World War II was a popular war against a common enemy. The reservists saved the Republic. It was a people's army and a people's Marine Corps. I had kids fifteen and sixteen years old in the Pacific who had lied about their age. You were supposed to be eighteen. They were pumped up, good and well trained. You asked if everything was so wonderful in World War II. Well, damn it, it was because everyone wanted to get the darn thing over with. Incidentally, the Pacific war was the only major war the United States ever won all by itself.

"Company commander—the rank of captain—is the best job for officers in the Marine Corps because the corps is a small-unit operation. Your basic control point is the company, from that spring your platoons and squads. Major is a half-baked rank, a nonrank. The marines have darn good leadership at regimental level downward. The strategy is obvious: you have to take the damn hill. And there aren't many ways you can take a hill. You can catch the enemy by surprise and take it. Or, if he's fully awake, you've got to divert him in one direction and hit him from the other. Or, if he's ready for everything, you've just got to *assault.* Your own mortars and artillery are firing ahead of you, and as soon as the range lengthens you move up behind it, the closer the better. In that kind of situation, that's where initiative and leadership count at squad and platoon level. The marines can *do* that; so can the best units in the army."

Hunt thinks tradition is important too. "When the band marches along and the flag is raised at dawn, and the band plays 'The Marine Corps Hymn,' it's a thrilling sound. Sousa composed some beauties, and they were often played in World War II. I think this is very important, especially at the beginning of training. The marine was not thinking of 'The Marine Corps Hymn' when he was dropping a grenade down the vent of a Japanese pillbox, but the hymn had a lot to do with getting him there. What keeps him going in the face of enemy fire? It narrows down to this: you don't let the other man down."

William Ketcham

Bill Ketcham sits in the third-floor dining room of the Brook Club in Manhattan, waiting for his portrait to be taken. Endowed with a full head of hair parted dead center, he is wearing a white Oxford shirt, a charcoal-gray suit with cuffs, and highly polished black wing-tip shoes. A former United States team squash player, Ketcham looks fit and spry for his years. The room is oak paneled with a single oil portrait; there are mullion windows with leaded panes, candelabra, and silver cups and trophies. In this setting, Ketcham looks—and is—the quintessential Yankee gentleman. It is hard to imagine him more than forty years before, filthy and bloody, leading his company of marines against heavily defended Japanese pillboxes on Iwo Jima. The scars are no longer visible, though shrapnel is still coming out of his knee. The memories live longer.

"I was at Yale at the time the draft was introduced," he begins, "and I discovered very quickly that I had one of the lowest numbers drawn out of the national lottery. You've probably seen some of those pictures of President Roosevelt and Secretary of the Navy Knox drawing the early numbers out of a great big drum. I won some money at Yale betting on a low number. I didn't really want to go into the army, and I didn't have the mathematics to go into the navy officer program. Then a marine officer, a great big guy dressed in blues, showed up on campus. I don't think I saw another set of blues until the war was over. He said he was going to take eight or ten men from Yale for officer training. I asked him who had been applying from here and of course four or five of them were big hotshots in our class. One of them was the best all-round athlete and another went on to be the Episcopal bishop of New York. I didn't have any previous family connection with the Marine Corps although Major General Smedley Butler was a great friend of my grandparents. Anyway, I got a couple of letters of recommendation, and I was selected.

"I went down to Quantico in January 1942 to what was then called the officer candidates class, the equivalent of boot camp. I was hopeless during the first half, not good at bayonet drill and that kind of thing. In the early part of the war they flunked a lot of people out. The Marine Corps was smaller than the New York City police force at that time. Later nobody got pushed out because they needed the bodies so much. The thing that saved me was shooting—always a big thing with the marines—and I happened to shoot very well so they couldn't really get rid of me then. We still used the old single-shot, bolt-action Springfield rifle, before changing to the M-1.

"Much to my amazement I was selected to stay as an instructor at Quantico. I guess they didn't want to trust me with troops yet. I was a teacher for two and a half years. When I was a candidate I had this great big Polish platoon sergeant on my tail the whole bloody time. After I had been reassigned as a teacher, I was standing out front with all my fancy stuff on—it was still boots and britches and Sam Brownes in those days—and he came out of the barracks and looked at me and said: 'Oooh, no!' Now I was going to be his boss. Actually, it turned out that we got along beautifully.

"Some people were constantly trying to get out to the Pacific before their time. I never did that because I thought I'd wait and see what they did to me. Also, it was pretty good duty down there with Washington close by, and we had a lot of fun. Then I was sent down to New River to join a replacement unit and on to Pendleton. Finally, we were put on board ship and ended up with the Fourth Division on Maui. They told me to report to the Third Battalion, Twenty-fourth Marines. The battalion commander was Archie Vandegrift with whom I'd worked at Quantico, and he gave me I Company. It was a rifle company with three rifle platoons and a weapons platoon, which was machine guns and mortars. General Cates, the hero of Guadalcanal, was the division commander.

"We did a lot of training on Maui. Our equipment wasn't too bad, and if we didn't have what we needed we'd steal it. I won an amphibious tank in a crap game once in Pearl Harbor, and when I tried to take it back to Maui we bogged down in the harbor. That was a very bad expedition. I also got chewed out by 'Howling Mad' Smith [General Holland M. Smith] while I was on Maui. He was a very gruff kind of a person. He up and asked me where some command post was. I didn't have the faintest idea, and I told him so. I said: 'General, I have no idea of where that command post is.' He said: 'Why you fucking son of a bitch, if you don't know where the command post is, I ought to relieve you right on the spot.'

"We knew something was coming but didn't know exactly what. They'd tell you on board ship a couple of days before you landed. The Fourth Division had already had a lot of battles. They'd been on Saipan and Tinian and had a big turnover. A lot of guys were killed and wounded so the division was a mix of guys who'd been through quite a bit plus new people. They were from all over the country, and I've always felt that the real end of the Civil War came in World War II when all these people from different regions were thrown in together and found that the guy from Alabama wasn't so bad and the guy from Iowa was OK. And as for us snotty Eastern liberals—we weren't even liberal in those days—it's probably the best thing that ever happened to us. Society was a lot more snobbish in those days. The war was, in that sense, very good for us all."

Ketcham pauses to light a cigar. "Iwo Jima really began for me when we were on board ship and saw all the naval gunfire going on, and they told us very categorically that we weren't going to have anything to do except just walk ashore. Of course, the Japs just pulled back into their caves and shut the door and the gunfire bounced off them and that was that. The Fourth Division went in on the right, with the Fifth Division on the left, and the Third stayed as reserve. Suribachi was in the Fifth Division's territory, and our division was across the airfield and all those hills on the right. We went in on D-Day plus two or something like that, but everyone was still on the beach. You could go up about twenty-five to fifty yards but that was it. The beach was black sulphurous sand. When you lay down at night your back would sweat because of the sulphur burning in the ground beneath you. But you'd have to put something warm on top because there it was very cold. The guys used to say that hell couldn't be any different from this. You had the stench of the sulphur, the fumes going up in the air, and then you got the stench of all the dead men, too. The first dead man I came across I turned over, and it was an officer I knew very well; we'd been at Quantico together. But after you'd seen a few you'd get pretty inured to it and didn't spend much time thinking about it."

Was there great confusion on the beach? "Yes and no. Confusion in the sense that everybody was trying to do different things and they were all attempting to reach different objectives. It was ordered confusion in another sense. To some degree you did things automatically, the way you'd trained to do them. You spent a lot of the time yelling at the guys to get down because if they stood up they were going to get shot. I think the biggest thing that training does when you are in a pretty darn scary situation is teach troops not to panic. Every so often in the battle you saw units suddenly leave their positions and start to retreat without really being told to. The pressure just got too much. But that didn't happen often. I suspect the highest mortality rate was among the second lieutenants, who were out there trying to lead their people. Most of my lieutenants were killed, and I got battlefield commissions for the NCOs who took over the platoons.

"You ran on nerve. You slept very spasmodically. Your day was never an ordered day. You might be in a hell of a fire fight for six or seven hours; the next day you might not hear a shot fired all day. Fortunately, everybody was pretty damn fit in those days. The training had done that.

"The casualty rate was extremely high. I had over 100 percent casualties in my company, killed or wounded, and we had to replace them during the twenty-eight-day period we were there. I was hit in the arm and the leg on two different occasions. What happened was," he stands up to demonstrate, "some Japanese with a machine gun zeroed in on me and got off the first two clips. I had ten bullet holes all the way down the side of my dungarees. One nicked my arm and the other my leg; the rest went straight through the dungarees. If he had traversed an inch or two over, I wouldn't be standing here now. Later on I got a shell or mortar fragment in my knee. I was luckier than John Lardner, the war correspondent who wrote for *The New Yorker*, who was hit in the groin on Iwo by what he thought was a fragment of stone. Several months later, back in New York, he was taking a shower and a small-caliber machine gun bullet worked its way out of his testicle and fell with a clunk on the floor.

"The worst thing was friends dying, some of them lying out there for a couple of days. You couldn't get to them, and you could hear them scream, and there was nothing you could do about it. The best thing was when you could see progress being made. It was vital to keep moving. The navy corpsmen were so wonderful, all over that battlefield, picking people up, with an almost reckless regard for their own safety. And then, of

course, the flag raising on Mount Suribachi. All of a sudden everybody heard some shouting. We looked around to where everybody was pointing, down to the left, and we saw the flag going up. That was a great morale booster."

How did he feel about the Japanese? "The interesting thing was you didn't have feelings about them," he says. "First, they were all in these caves and underground tunnels. The whole island was a network of tunnels so you very seldom saw any of them. Every so often you'd come across a dead one here and there; but you rarely saw a live one. Twenty thousand Japanese died in the battle, and very few prisoners were taken. They were obstacles—nothing you could really relate to except as goddamn Japs."

Ketcham puffs reflectively at his cigar. He says he learned to smoke cigars in the Marine Corps as part of the tough-guy image in those days.

"After the battle was over," he continues, "Admiral Nimitz said that uncommon valor was a common virtue. After all those guys had been killed I guess he had to say something."

Did he go back? "No, but I wish I had," he says. "I never had any personal problems about dealing with the Japanese. I spent a lot of time in Japan on business in postwar years, and I never dreamed about the battle either. It was just something I had to do, and I was lucky to come through. The big difference between World War II and all the others was that it was everybody's war. We were taught from the very first day we joined that we were better than anyone else. We were marines, right? So if you began to believe that, you were one up. And the kids believed it. I remember there was a little corporal in my company, and whenever the guys would go off on liberty, there'd be army guys here and there, and they'd always end up in fights of one sort or another. This corporal, a skinny little fella, had been picked up and brought back. He'd had the hell beat out of him. So he came in and I said, 'Jackson, what happened now?' 'Oh, Captain, it weren't no real problem,' he said. 'I got into an argument with five or six army guys, and I was lickin' the hell out of them until one got behind me.'" Ketcham laughs. "He *actually thought* he could beat six guys; that idea was built into him.

"I thought of staying on in the Marine Corps, and the only reason I didn't was because all the guys I liked were getting out. I had a bunch of these medals so it was very tempting to stay on. They offered me a regular commission. I often thought later that if I'd stayed, I would have probably been killed in Korea."

Ketcham joined the foreign service and was sent to London as a special assistant to the chairman of the North Atlantic Treaty Organization. He met Winston Churchill, who, on one occasion, gave him one of his monstrous cigars, which Ketcham still keeps, resisting the temptation to smoke it. Another time he was in the men's room in the House of Commons, which had just been renovated. "Who should come in to the very next stall but Churchill," he says. "I was a young flustered kid and didn't know what the hell to say. So I said something about the renovated building like 'Oh, isn't this all so lovely, Mr. Prime Minister?' He looked at me and said: 'Young man, it certainly makes me ashamed of my shabby old cock.'"

Does the Navy Cross have a special meaning to marines? "I guess it does," says Ketcham. "I was very honored to get it, and people seemed impressed. Why is it special? Well, it's second only to the Congressional Medal of Honor, and then some famous marines won it such as 'Chesty' Puller [he won *five* of them]. General Cates got it in World War I. Marines like to make a little thing out of quote valor unquote. That's their trademark."

Here is an extract from Ketcham's Navy Cross citation:

When the advance was held up by devastating enemy fire, he ordered his forces to take cover and with complete disregard for his own safety moved alone over some two hundred yards of exposed terrain to a rocky crest forward of his right flank platoon from which, in spite of heavy mortar and small arms fire aimed at his position, he directed accurate 60mm mortar and artillery fire on four pillboxes to his direct front.

Ketcham's own summary of his World War II experience is precise and simple. "I don't think you could have a better thing in the world than to be commanding officer of a company of marines in that war," he says. "I think I was a very lucky guy."

Robert Sherrod, who covered the battle for *Time* magazine, wrote the following passage six days after the initial assault:

The ultimate factor in the fall of Iwo Jima will be the character and courage of the U.S. Marine Corps. There comes a time when defenses will no longer yield before fire power, however heavy. That is the time when men on foot must pay for yardage with their lives. That is when the marines are at their greatest. This, said the Fleet Marine Force commander, Lieutenant General Holland M. ("Howlin' Mad") Smith, is their toughest fight in 168 years.

Along the beach in the morning lay many dead. About them, whether American or Jap, there was one thing in common. They died with the greatest possible violence. Nowhere in the Pacific war have I seen such badly mangled bodies. Many were cut squarely in half. Legs and arms lay fifty feet away from any body. Only the legs were easy to identify—Japanese if wrapped in khaki puttees, American if covered by canvas leggings. In one spot of the sand, far from the nearest clusters of dead men, I saw a string of guts 15 feet long.

At the end of his story, which appeared in *Time* magazine on March 5, 1945, Sherrod made a prediction. "My strictly unofficial estimate is that the conquest of Iwo Jima will take 13 days, and that casualties will be slightly less than on Saipan (3,147 killed and missing; 13,054 wounded)." Sherrod, a fine reporter, was sadly mistaken. It took the marines thirty-six days to conquer the sulphur island and, in doing so, 6,821 were killed and 19,030 were wounded.

Raymond Murray

Major General Murray lives in a pleasant villa in Oceanside, California, close to Camp Pendleton. "I retired here because I like being close to the Marine Corps," he says in a rich, gravelly voice. He plays golf three times a week and works in the yard a bit. Remarkably fit and alert for a man of seventy-five with one lung, he stopped smoking when he saw the X-rays of the diseased organ. "It was a mishmash," he says, "so I quit smoking." His living room is full of military memorabilia. There are pictures of him with Douglas MacArthur, George Bush (a congressman during the Korean War), John Kennedy, Mark Clark, Chiang Kai-Shek, and other notables. In a glass case is a marvelous collection of his campaign medals, which is framed by the brim of his uniform hat and its globe and anchor badge. It was put together locally by a former marine colonel and was a present from his wife. The inscription reads: "For Ray Forevermore, Love, Helen, 30 January, 1974." There is also a glass display case of Zippo lighters, many of them embellished with the Marine Corps emblem. Murray joined the corps in 1935 when there was a total of thirteen generals. He served in China from 1938 to 1940. He fought at Guadalcanal, Tarawa, and Saipan, where he won his first Navy Cross. In Korea he commanded the Fifth Marines and won his second Navy Cross and the army's Distinguished Service Cross in the retreat from the Chosin Reservoir. He ended his career in another war as deputy commander III Marine Amphibious Force in Vietnam.

"I went to Texas A & M and graduated in 1935," he says. "I was planning to teach school and hoped one day to get into school administration and maybe wind up as a school superintendent somewhere. A month before I graduated, the professor of military science and tactics, the head military man at A & M, called me into his office and asked me if I'd like to be a marine. I said, 'I don't know, sir, what's a marine?' He said: 'Well, it's a small outfit but a good military operation. We can nominate one principal and one alternate and all you have to do is pass the physical, and then you get a regular commission in the Marine Corps.' I asked for a little time to think about it and went back and tried to read everything I could about the Marine Corps. But there was virtually nothing in the library or any other place. However, after talking to some of my friends and professors, I decided to give it a try because I found out it paid $125 a month, twelve months a year, whereas my teaching prospects were for $90 a month for nine months a year. I got orders, went to Philadelphia [Basic School] without a penny to my name and with only the clothes I was wearing. I said, 'So here I am, ready to be a marine.' I had thought if there were a war, I'd stay through that and then get out. But you've heard of the Marine Corps brainwashing bit. Well, about two weeks after I arrived in Philadelphia they would have had to put a big charge under me to get me out of the corps. I was sold on it and have been sold ever since."

He gets up and lets a nervous cat out the door into the garden. "If war can be fun," he continues, "Korea was a fun war to fight in the sense that there were lots of maneuvers, lots of being on your own, no one on your flanks, sometimes nobody in your rear. It was an interesting type of fighting; we did just about everything a military organization can do during the year that I was there. We made an amphibious landing [at Inchon]; we did a river crossing; we fought in a big built-up city [Seoul]; we fought in the mountains in extreme cold; and we fought a withdrawal action [Chosin]. We were able to use a lot of initiative and do some of the maneuvering that we learned when we went to school but that we didn't use in WWII. Most of that war was fought on islands, where you simply landed against the opposition, butted your head against the wall, and pulled and pushed until you got to the other side.

"Korea was altogether different, at least in the early days. It was exciting, too, because of the Inchon landing. That was especially interesting because most of us thought it was a stupid idea to land where the tides were thirty feet. You went in on one tide, got as much ashore as you could and then had to wait twelve hours before another tide came in. As it turned out, of course, it was a brilliant idea, as many of General MacArthur's ideas were. He was like Fiorello La Guardia, the mayor of New York: he didn't make many mistakes but when he did they were beauties.

"The marines were ready to fight that kind of war. My unit, the Fifth Marines, made the landing at Inchon on Red Beach. We did some very heavy fighting in the perimeter at Pusan and then broke out. We were later pushed back inside it but we forced our way out again and broke a North Korean division. I was in an observation post overlooking a hill and saw the Koreans break. They just picked up and ran, and we were shooting at them with everything we had. I was jumping up and down at the top of this hill yelling and shouting every time I saw another round catch another North Korean, or a tank round blow a bunch of people up into the air. It was very exciting.

"Another thrilling thing about the fighting in Korea was that the troops were so great. We had a lot of veteran NCOs from World War II, but most of the privates and even the young corporals were post-World War II. They were mostly kids eighteen or nineteen years old. The previous commander of the Fifth Marines, Victor 'Brute' Krulak, had trained the regiment beautifully, and the reserves also did well. So we had a great bunch of men. There was nothing like what you heard of later in Vietnam. These were people who believed in what they were doing and did a marvelous job. A regiment is a great command, and there is a special mystique attached to the unit you fought with. In Korea I used to take the radio man in a jeep with a driver, pick out a hill, and run the war from there. I could see the whole regiment and battlefield down below me."

General Murray's second Navy Cross was awarded for his role in the famous breakout from the Chosin Reservoir in North Korea in the bitter winter of 1950. "We had been surrounded by massive numbers of Chinese," he says, "and fought our way back to Hagaru as a unit and later moved back to Kota-ri. They decided that it was worth a Navy

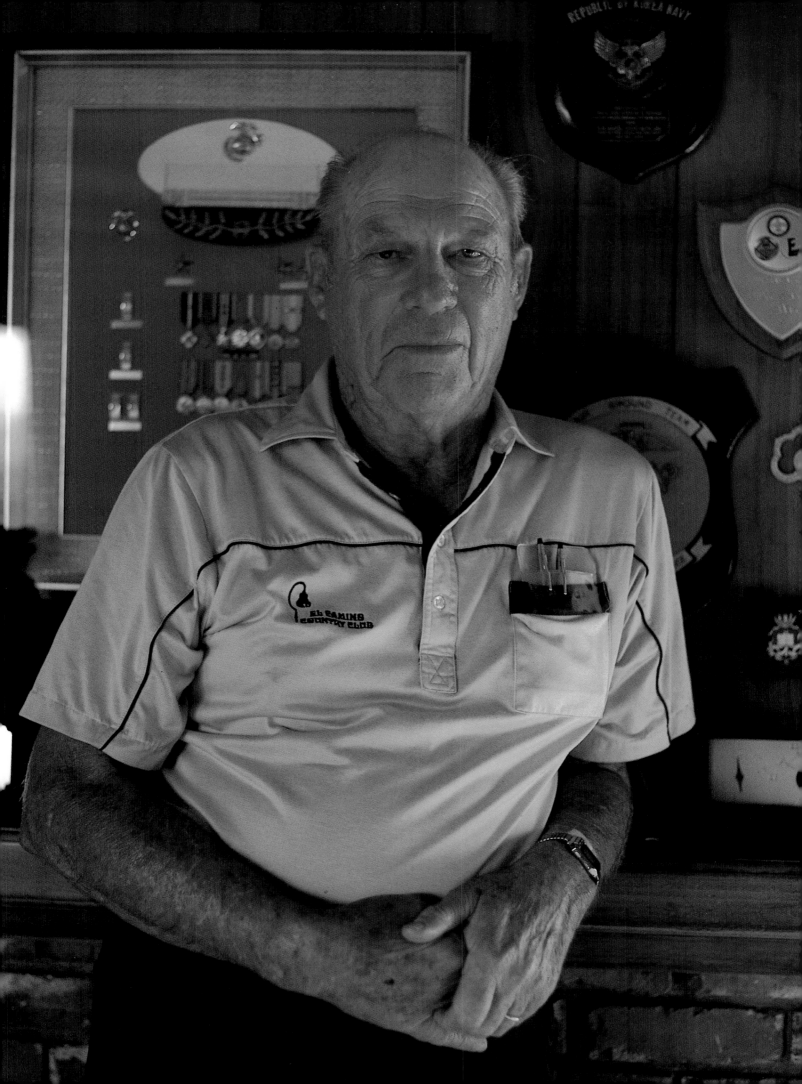

Cross. I didn't do anything other than issue the orders." He chuckles. "But I had some troops who could carry out the orders so that is what it was for. I don't really know what or who deserves a Navy Cross or a Silver Star. I know a lot of people got them for doing just what I did—issuing orders that are carried out properly. If that's worth it, well, fine."

Looking back on his campaigns in three major wars, Murray comments: "If I had to go to war again, I would like to do it with the people I went to war with in Korea. They were great people."

Martin Brandtner

The colonel's office is in the original wooden building that housed the headquarters of the First Marine Division in Camp Pendleton when it was formed in 1942. There is a division plaque with its constellation of the Southern Cross and "Guadalcanal" insignia on the wall, and walking along the creaking polished wood corridors, you can, if you close your eyes for a moment, almost hear Glenn Miller's band riffing away on an old radio down the hallway.

Colonel Brandtner, a stocky man who thinks before he speaks, wears Vietnam on his chest. He was awarded two Navy Crosses, a Legion of Merit with Combat "V," and a Purple Heart. He has just been selected for brigadier general. "Fooled 'em again," he says with a grin. "Now they're telling me to come to Washington to be taught how to eat.

"I think the marines performed magnificently in Vietnam under extremely arduous circumstances," he says. "They were there during the entire war and fought some of its fiercest battles. They were stationed in the northern I Corps area and fought both the VC and straight-line North Vietnam army units. The North Vietnamese were very competent soldiers—highly trained and well disciplined. But toe for toe, man for man, they couldn't match the marines.

"We had some disciplinary problems but not in line units. There just wasn't the time or the occasion. A marine who was going to get into trouble didn't do it in combat. But we had undercurrents of racial tension back in Da Nang. We did not have the proliferation of 'fragging' [the wounding or killing of officers by their own troops] incidents in the Marine Corps that I'd heard about in other places. I can only recall one incident in the entire time I spent there. It was regarded by all as a gross tragedy. A disaffected marine committed an act of murder, without collusion of his mates, and it was treated as such."

Another officer had told us that Vietnam was in the marines' psyche, whether they liked it or not. What did he think?

"Yes, I agree, but I would suggest that as marines such as myself grow older— I've served in the Marine Corps for twenty-eight years; I'm almost a dinosaur—the vast number of young marines today don't know anything about Vietnam except what they are told or what they read. You have lieutenant colonels, battalion commanders, for example, who did not serve in Vietnam. But the senior officers and staff NCOs are still affected by Vietnam. Marines as an institution are extremely wary of committing national resources to a conflict or an operation that doesn't have the support of the American public. We saw at the end of the war and when I came home that we were doing something that really wasn't popular. We felt betrayed—I think that's a fair word—and many marines I know still feel that Americans haven't truly appreciated what really happened over there or have a real sense of the historical perspective that the war placed on things. And maybe they never will."

Few military men like to talk about how they won their valor awards, and the colonel is no exception. But he is not only a brave man, he is also a polite one and, under pressure, gives a little ground. This is how he won his two Navy Crosses.

"I was company commander of Company D. We were operating in the An Hoa Basin in the 'Arizona' area, and we had been having a series of skirmishes with the Twenty-first North Vietnamese Army Regiment. We were moving a lot at night and would leave positions and go back to them the following night. The NVA had a habit of coming back and occupying places where we had been, scavenging and generally trying to disrupt our activity. Thinking we would continue to move on, they would occupy our rear and then attack us from that direction. So we would try to keep them off balance. On this particular occasion we moved at about one o'clock in the morning and conducted a predawn assault. I had just one company, and we discovered that we were head to head with at least a battalion. Things got pretty heavy. A lot of grenades were flying around, and a lot were flying back. The marines around me were under a tremendous siege and I, along with others who were later decorated, took the offensive just to stem the tide.

"It was a fierce battle. All of us were wounded at least once. Thanks to the aggressiveness of a couple of platoon commanders on my flanks, along with my element of the command, we were able to overcome the enemy resistance. During the fray a number of grenades landed around me and my command group. It was almost like a snowball fight. Finally, a grenade landed in the middle of a bunch of marines, and I could see that they were all going to be killed, so I just did what I had to do." He pauses.

What *did* he do?

"I threw the grenade back. It blew up in the air but I had gotten on top of them before it went off so the injuries were minor. They were grateful enough to cite me for the award.

"The other occasion was in a battle about eight days later, not far from the previous area. We had moved into a position just before dark, and our intention was to tie a flank up to the river and set up in a position to allow us to do some night patrolling along the river. We knew that the NVA would cross at various points, and we were going to set up ambushes to try to stop them from crossing. It had rained tremendously over the past weeks, and what had happened, unknown to us, was that the river had actually split a little, flooded a lower area, and isolated a piece of high ground that turned out to be the command post of the Twenty-first Regiment. We thought we were on the edge of the river whereas we were actually on that little strip of ground. So we set up our position, and as soon as it got dark I sent off a couple of combat patrols. But before they left, my platoon commander was shot, and the patrol was ambushed.

"When we popped illumination up in the air, I looked out over the river that I thought was twenty-five or thirty feet deep. But it wasn't. The water was only ankle to knee deep. And there were two to three hundred NVA troops coming across at us in a line. We fought off two or three human wave attacks, and the battle went on through the night. We were resupplied—a tremendous effort by marine helicopters under intense fire—and we decided in the end that the only option left was to attack. So we fixed bayonets and went after 'em. And we succeeded. I had about seventy-five marines with me. I don't have any idea what numbers of enemy—three or four hundred maybe—but when we finished we had one killed and fifteen wounded seriously enough to be evacuated. There were at least eighty Vietnamese dead on the battlefield that we knew about, plus those who left and the ones they dragged away. But I want to make clear that this was not a one-man show. There were a hell of a lot of wonderful, wonderful marines."

Colonel Brandtner was James Webb's executive officer in the First Battalion, Fifth Marines, in Vietnam. Webb later went on to become Secretary of the Navy for a short period; but in *Fields of Fire,* his gripping and poignant novel about Vietnam, Webb was critical of the American military command.

"I think a lot of his criticism was justified," Brandtner says, "but I also note the tremendous pride he had in the ordinary marine, and I think that truly reflected the kind of people we had in that battalion and the corps at the time. Reading his novel was an emotional thing for me. I knew the 'Arizona' area that he describes and bled a bit over that land myself."

And the modern marine?

"The marine of today is different in many respects, but he's also the same as his forebears," Brandtner says. "He's a lot better informed. He's confronted with a lot more temptations. Society and its values are vastly different today. But, as far as his motivation is concerned, I don't think there's a great deal of difference. I have often spoken with World War II veterans who, I might add, take issue with the fact that people will say the marine of today is a better man. I maintain that there were some pretty good marines who took Suribachi. The same kind of man fought in Hue City. He was motivated largely by the same kind of things.

"What motivates a marine is the same as it has been throughout history. It is a pride in his unit. It's a camaraderie with his fellow marine. A sense of peer love that means he is not going to let his fellow marines down. And there as a backdrop is patriotism and love of country, which certainly permeate his psyche. So that is not different. The modern marine is perhaps a little more self-oriented than his predecessor, but I wouldn't say they are better than their predecessors. They are better educated, and we don't have the disciplinary problems we had in the seventies. But then we didn't have those problems in the early sixties or before either. You have to see the seventies as an anomaly."

Has the civilian been taken out of the modern marine?

"I personally hope we never take the civilian out of the marine. We're Americans first and foremost and I take great pride in the fact that I am a native of this country—a Minnesotan—and I vote and do those things that are part of civilian life. I think the worst thing that could happen is that we would isolate ourselves from our own society and become mercenary, fighting simply for the sake of fighting."

James Webb

If there is a marines' marine in the modern era, it has to be James Webb, the heavily decorated Vietnam veteran who became the marines' civilian boss for a short period toward the end of the Reagan administration. The imposing office that belongs to the Secretary of the Navy in the Pentagon almost reeks marine in combat mode. A copy of *Life* magazine, the one that had a picture of an exhausted infantryman on the cover (June 27, 1969) and focused on one week's American dead in Vietnam, lies on the coffee table. A Vietcong flag, captured by Webb and his marines in "Arizona Valley," is in a glass case on the wall. A bronze miniature of the Vietnam War Memorial—the infantry trio—that Webb was largely responsible for bringing into being is on his conference table. A clay model of Webb's own combat boot, used for the memorial, resides on his desk. A World War II carbine, issued to the French army in Vietnam, reposes in another glass cabinet. Marines will tell you there are two different ways in which they view Vietnam: as a passing, albeit unforgettable, experience or as something that they feel in the marrow of their bones every day of their lives. Webb, who wrote a passionate novel about his experiences in Vietnam called *Fields of Fire,* is clearly in the second category.

The first Naval Academy graduate and combat veteran to become Secretary of the Navy, Webb is a small, trim man. In Vietnam he won the Navy Cross, the Silver Star, two Bronze Stars, and a Purple Heart. His wounds ended his career in the Marine Corps, but he went on to become a lawyer, a successful novelist, a congressional activist in veterans' affairs, a journalist—he covered the destruction of the marines' bunker in Beirut for the "MacNeil-Lehrer Report"—and a high functionary in the Pentagon. He became secretary of the navy at forty-one years old, and he looks ten years younger.

Why did he join the Marine Corps? "My father was an air force officer," he says.

"I went to many different schools and didn't have a stellar record from high school. I knew I wanted to go into the military. I liked the ground side because it was very physical, and I fell in love with the corps. If you want to be an intellectual giant you go to Yale. If you really want to be with the absolute best, you go into the Marine Corps. There's a tremendous psychic energy in the marines, there always has been. It was truly one of the greatest moments of my life when I was commissioned as a marine. There is a real purity in command, and the most rewarding experience I had in the corps was being a rifle company commander."

What does Vietnam mean to him?

"I never believed that Vietnam would fold. I thought that there would eventually be a negotiated settlement. Such an emotional experience at such an impressionable time in your life, it is hard to box it up and put it away. It's not the driving force in my life, but it is a part of my life. It's like my first marriage, which is part of my life too.

"The marines' casualty ratio was double that of any other service in Vietnam. We had over 103,000 killed or wounded. Almost a quarter of the marines who went west of Hawaii were killed or wounded, twice as many as in the army. The corps took more casualties in Vietnam than it did in World War II by 13,000, and had a higher casualty rate: 24 percent in Vietnam compared with 22 percent in World War II, though more actually died in the latter because of poorer medical facilities.

"We're still sorting out how Vietnam affected the Marine Corps. What is clear is that the reputation of the Marine Corps in Vietnam was salvaged by the privates and corporals and second lieutenants, the guys who did all the dying, not by doctrinal excellence. We went into Vietnam with a lot of wrong gear and wrong ideas. The Marine Corps did pretty damn well considering what was going on back home. And on the battlefield we did exceptionally well. One of the problems though is that in a nonwar, nonpeace environment, the U.S. leads with its chin. We put our military people out there, and then we try to develop diplomatic assurances. The British always do it the other way around. The quality of the marines was superb, but the army had horrendous problems in Vietnam."

What does he think about recruit training?

"The Marine Corps still does it better than anyone else," he says. "The commandant was right when he said that the ability to run three miles in a pair of sneakers does not mean you can carry a wounded guy across a parking lot. The major difference between the marines and most other major military systems that I've looked at is that the Marine Corps takes the same kid off the same block as the army and develops his *attitude*. You teach a person to be a marine, and then you teach him a skill. Attitudes are developed early, and they're very difficult to redevelop. So if you teach the right attitude about discipline, obligation, and accountability to the people around you and to the institution that you serve, then you can teach the skill. One reason there are so many successful former marines in our society is that you can take that attitude and use it to compete in other environments. That's the most important part of training, and it happens at boot camp and Officer Candidates School."

Webb says that he has heard about the DIs' complaints. He says he is concerned about them and about the ease with which recruits can quit.

"Some good people might have stayed if things had been tough enough to create the conditions where the guy couldn't quit," he says. "Physical fitness by itself does not mean tenacity. The thing that really disturbs me is the drill instructor being made to stand in front of his platoon and swear that he's going to be nice and not use bad language. That DI's got to be a god when he walks in there. It's up to the series commander to make sure that he doesn't abuse anyone. The officers aren't the problem, Congress is the problem and the American Civil Liberties Union lawyers."

Webb has firm ideas on officer training, too. His thinking is reflected in *Fields of Fire* when his second lieutenant hero, Bob Hodges, muses on the phenomenon of "fragging" in Vietnam: "Remembering the stories from Basic School, he [Hodges]

understood immediately why an individual would want to wound an incompetent officer with a grenade. It's not vindictiveness, he reasoned. It's self-preservation."

Webb has views on Naval Academy graduates in the Marine Corps. He thinks there are two problems. "First there is the socialization problem," he says. "They are marine officers, but they haven't felt the hands of a DI. Then there is the question: Are they ready to become marine officers? The Basic School at Quantico is an excellent measure of how prepared people are. Naval Academy guys did extremely well at TBS in my day. [Webb was his class honor man.] But the Naval Academy indoctrination program has been *grossly* diluted. The result is that you can multiply boot camp's problems by ten.

"When I went through the academy I could turn to OCS people and say I had spent a year doing five times worse stuff than they did at OCS. Up to the late seventies, Naval Academy people always graduated in the top half of the TBS classes. But from the late seventies onward, they've gone down; in 1986 they averaged the bottom fortieth percentile. These are guys who have just spent four years getting ready to go. The result is that I am going to have Naval Academy guys go through 'bulldog' [summer training at Officer Candidates School]. There are a number of people who go into the Marine Corps from the Naval Academy for the wrong reasons—to guarantee they get flying training, to avoid going to sea—people who are negatively motivated.

"The quota from the Naval Academy to the Marine Corps has changed from 8 percent in the sixties to 10 percent in the seventies, and now it's 16.6 percent. They do it by academic class standing, and that has very little to do with how well you will perform or even or how smart you are. So much of the curriculum is hard science."

Webb once wrote a critical article on women in the military that brought much wrath upon his head.

"I'm not against women in the military," he says, "but against females in *combat,* in a high-tempo operating unit. My wife spent five years in the army. But when you get units that are operational, isolated, and what I call labor intensive, where unit cohesion is the driving force, you want to have the right set of folks out there doing it. You end up with a lot of problems when you mix those units male and female."

Webb covered the Beirut disaster as a journalist and has this to say about the incident.

"The marines were superb," he says, "but the political and diplomatic process screwed it up. It was a 'can't-shoot-back' charade. In order to return fire the marines had to identify their opponent, his weapon, then shoot back with a similar weapon and for a short time. In other words, 'semimilitary rules' applied. Marines were not allowed to dig in until they started receiving artillery rounds. After the bunker blew up, they took better defensive action. Colonel Geraghty [the unit commander], a good marine, shouldn't have been court-martialed, as some critics suggested, but he could have said, "Look, unless you give me proper support and allow my men to defend themselves, I'll quit.'"

Shortly after becoming Secretary of the Navy, Webb was quoted as saying that the marines had an identity crisis. "What I meant," he says, "was in terms of doctrine. Where the hell are they going? Are they amphibious or capable of sustaining long-term operations? We are in danger of building a program that's designed for amphibious power projection that will have complications when it has to switch over to sustained ground combat. We went through this in Vietnam. The marine helicopter CH-46 was designed for limited deck space with two allocated per regiment. Whereas the army had developed the air mobile concept better than we had with eight helicopters per company, making their troops highly maneuverable. We ran two helicopters per regiment on a typical day. So we walked, and when you walk you take more casualties. That's the identity crisis."

When the commandant made a comment about the Marine Corps being "broken" and needing "fixing," what did he think?

"The Marine Corps is different," Webb says. "People expect it to be absolutely beyond cavil, the best. I don't think that the corps is broken in any fundamental way. I believe that the Marine Corps is the finest ground combat force, man for man, in the world, and I've seen just about all of them that have any claim to being good. But the political environment in which we force marines to operate is often quite a problem. There are things they need to do to get better. Part of that is initial training, attitude development; part of it is sorting out doctrine—those things are going to be worked on. The Marine Corps is not hurt as badly as some people say. The average marine and the average American are not worried. But the Lonetree thing hurt most; the idea that marines could betray their country really hurts.

"The Marine Corps is pretty big. The corps is one third larger than the British army but has only one fifth of its general officers. And there's no one in the world who can do the combined arms types of things that any marine rifle platoon commander can do. As one in Vietnam, I could pick up the hook and personally direct mortar, artillery, close air support, talk to beacon hops, et cetera. Now we're teaching squad leaders to do all that. There's not an individual in the Israeli army who knows how to call in close air support, so the Marine Corps ain't that bad."

Summing up, Webb quotes a sentence in an article entitled "Success in War," written by George Patton in 1931, when he was a major.

"'It is the gleam in the attacker's eye and not the glitter of the bayonet that breaks the line . . . and yet volumes are devoted to armament and pages to inspiration.'"

"It's attitude that sustains a fighting person," says Webb, "and that's why the Marine Corps has always been so good."

Richard Pittman

The officers who had won the Navy Cross all made the point that their awards reflected the valor and steadfastness of their men, that the decoration belonged to their troops as much as to themselves. While we were in Camp Pendleton in California we came across an enlisted marine who had won a personal award for valor, the highest in the land. He was Master Sergeant Richard A. Pittman in the Provost Marshal's office, and he had a story to tell.

There are a dwindling number of Medal of Honor winners still serving in the Marine Corps, a half dozen at the most. The nation's highest award for valor, "above and beyond the call of duty," is a simple decoration: a five-pointed star with a cluster of white stars on a pale blue ribbon. But on dress blues there is no missing it since it is the only medal worn around the neck. It would be hard to miss it anyway, given the knowledge that it is only awarded for acts of extreme bravery, more of them posthumously than to living recipients, and with great parsimony.

Master Sergeant Pittman's moment came on July 24, 1966, when he was a lance corporal in the first platoon of I Company, Third Battalion, Fifth Marines, near the DMZ in Vietnam. With five uncles who had been marines, he says it was expected by his family that he would join the corps. But he had a problem. He had been blind in his right eye since the age of five so he had to get into the service by "other than normal means." He made it by joining the reserves and cheating on the eye exam.

"The corpsman told me to cover my right eye, the bad one, and read the chart with my left eye," he says lighting up a cigarette. "Knowing that I was going to have to cover my left eye and read the chart, instead of covering my right eye with my right hand, I covered it with my left and read the chart again. And so I passed the eye test.

"The Marine Corps didn't find out about it until two and a half years later, when I was in Vietnam. I was transferred from the infantry to a motor transport unit as a tractor-trailer driver for tactical convoys. Somebody came up with this regulation that said we must have a medical certificate to haul explosives in a combat zone. I never understood that one, but I took an eye test and they were a little more proficient, I guess, and caught me. I was medically discharged after I came back to the States. But about eighteen months after I was decorated and had had several differences of opinion with civilian employers, I asked the commandant if I could come back into the Marine Corps, and they waived the eye requirements. That was January 1970, and I've been here ever since."

It was on Operation Hastings in July 1966 that Pittman first found himself in direct contact with North Vietnamese army regulars. He was a fire-team leader at the time and says he was trained and ready for combat. "I don't know if we were naive, but we believed in the war," he says. "Our fathers were veterans of World War II, and it was our job to fight. We were ambushed on the night of July 23 and suffered some casualties. The next morning we were ordered to move to Hill 362 to act as a radio relay for the other battalions and supporting arms. As we were moving up the hill in a company column on the morning of July 24, we were ambushed by two North Vietnamese battalions. The point platoon was almost wiped out, and we lost all of our M-60s except one. My platoon was in the rear of the column so when the ambush started we stopped, set up a defensive perimeter, and attempted to get the wounded and everybody back and set up a base of fire.

"I could hear people calling for more fire ahead from the kill zone. There was a marine sitting next to me on the edge of the perimeter with the M-60 machine gun. I asked him if he was going to use the gun, and he said no. So I picked up the gun and several belts of ammunition and went down the trail. I took out a couple of enemy automatic weapons positions on the way. A corpsman went with me but he was killed. As I got to the front of the ambush, the North Vietnamese apparently thought we were done so they sent about forty people in a frontal assault to overrun us, and I stopped the assault. They came twice. I was just lucky."

Was he wounded?

"Nope. I had my helmet shot off and a bullet stuck in one of the brass snaps of my cartridge belt, believe it or not. The gun took two rounds and was shot out of my hands so I picked up an AK-47. It was them or me. They got us in a classic ambush, but we killed about three hundred of them. I was just lucky, I guess."

The citation was more specific: "Taken under intense enemy small-arms fire at point-blank range during his advance, Sergeant (then Lance Corporal) Pittman returned fire, silencing the enemy positions. As he continued to forge forward to aid members of the leading platoon, he again came under heavy fire from two automatic weapons which he promptly destroyed. Learning that there were additional wounded Marines fifty yards farther along the trail, he braved a withering hail of enemy mortar and small-arms fire to continue onward. As he reached the position where the leading Marines had fallen, he was suddenly confronted with a bold frontal attack by thirty or forty enemy. Totally disregarding his own safety, he calmly established a position in the middle of the trail and raked the advancing enemy with devastating machine-gun fire. His weapon rendered ineffective, he picked up an enemy submachine gun and together with a pistol seized from a fallen comrade continued his lethal fire until the enemy force had withdrawn. Having exhausted his ammunition except for a grenade which he hurled at the enemy, he than rejoined his own platoon. . . ."

Not bad for a guy with one eye.

Pittman knew that he was being considered for a Navy Cross. But he heard nothing more about the affair for another two years. He gives a matter-of-fact account: "By that time I had been discharged from the Marine Corps because of my bad eye and was looking for a job. One day there was a knock on my door, and a marine lieutenant colonel, accompanied by two staff NCOs, told me that I had been awarded the Medal of Honor and that the President would like me to come to Washington."

IWO JIMA

United States Marines are back on Iwo Jima—not many, not often, and without fanfare. But they are back. Japanese sensitivities—the island was returned to Japan in 1978—preclude more than the occasional visit or exercise. The vanquished are still disinterring their dead, still finding bodies, occasionally coming across macabre tableaux like the hospital cave with skeletons lying on stretchers, splints still in place, and intravenous drips still attached—or the party of schoolchildren who visited the island on a botany trip and were caught in the battle. They were given two grenades each, one to kill an American, the other to kill themselves. But, as the evidence of the caves suggests, they did not obey orders and were killed by their own kind.

One marine who went back, Colonel John W. Ripley, spent a lonely vigil on the top of Mount Suribachi. It was cold and wet, but he wrote a letter to a friend back home, holding a flashlight under his chin. This is what he said:

From this most unlikely spot I am inspired to write you for reasons I can't really explain. Certainly you have received no other letters from here I would wager, and you may find this interesting. It's the middle of the night—cold, windy, and uncomfortable and profoundly moving. I'm looking down on a tiny island three miles wide and five miles long. Down there, and here where I'm writing by flashlight, over 7,000 Marines died. The mountain is Suribachi, the island, Iwo Jima. Of the hundreds of thousands of words written about this place nothing comes close to describing its starkness, its inestimable cost, and now, sadly, the poverty of its abandonment.

The entire island is a shrine; most Japanese, but a few American—only a few. Americans don't seem to care about such things when, as is the case here, it's inconvenient. And yet this island, its name, and, most especially this very spot where I sit—where the flag was raised—is immortalized in our national consciousness for as long as there is an America.

The debris and detritus of war remain even after nearly forty-three years. Rusted vehicle hulks, wrecked boats, sunken ships, canteens, mess kits, thousands of rounds of corroded ammunition, blockhouses, pillboxes, trenches, abandoned airfields, large naval shore guns, artillery, etc. And beneath my feet the remains of 22,000 Japanese defenders, brave men who died at their posts; hated then, respected now.

Rupert Brooke said it perfectly: "Here, in some small corner of a forgotten field, will be forever England." And this brutally stinking sulfuric rock, depressing to see, demoralizing as it has lost its once vital importance and our nation's once great concern, will be forever America. It will be forever in the memory of those 75,000 Marines who fought here, the 25,000 who suffered wounds here and the 7,000 who gave their blood and lives to its black soil. Again Rupert Brooke . . . "In that rich earth, a richer dust concealed." Their hopes, their happiness, their dreams ended here. And if we fail to honor them in our memory and our prayers we should be damned to hell for such failure.

CODA: THE STATE OF THE MARINE CORPS

As the last decade of the twentieth century approaches, the United States Marine Corps appears to be in good shape. The Reagan administration's military build-up brought a bonanza of new weapons and equipment, and, even allowing for some planned reductions in manpower, the corps' strength will continue to hover near the two hundred thousand mark. The quality of its recruits, especially their educational levels, continues to be high. The corps is adapting to the likelihood that there will be more small Third World skirmishes to fight than large conventional wars. Marines hitting the beach are likely to be reconnaissance marines or small "special operations capable" units rather than regiments or divisions. Congress in particular and the American public in general seem content with the state of the Marine Corps. There are no major complaints, no major threats.

There has, however, been a rough passage. Former California Congressman Pete McCloskey, a marine veteran of the Korean War, summed it up: "When I saw two-hundred-plus marines in Beirut bunched up in violation of every standard precept, I winced," he said. "When I saw Ollie North, I winced. And Moscow. It just killed us."

On October 23, 1983, a terrorist with a smile on his face drove a Mercedes truck loaded with explosives into the marines' bunker near the Beirut airport. The truck exploded, and 241 marines died, most of them in their beds. When the scandal involving the secret sale of U.S. arms to Iran and the diversion of the profits to the "contra" rebels in Central America broke in Washington in late 1985, it was revealed that two marines — Oliver North, still on active duty; and Robert "Bud" McFarlane, retired — were deeply involved. In the spring of 1987, Sergeant Clayton Lonetree, who had served in the Marine Security Guard detachment in the U.S. embassy in Moscow, was charged with spying for the Soviet Union. Other marines in Moscow and elsewhere had disciplinary action taken against them for lesser offenses.

In all these incidents investigations, inquiries, and post-mortems were performed by the Marine Corps and others. The storm of criticism and publicity that attended each event gradually died down, and the wounds slowly healed. But in each case the marines' hierarchy seemed reluctant to take decisive action to establish where blame truly lay, reluctant perhaps to be seen washing its dirty linen in public and thus attracting even more attention to the corps' problems. The Beirut disaster was blamed on the politicians. Oliver North kept his job — and his security clearances — in Marine Corps headquarters until he was actually indicted for theft and fraud. The commander of the Marine Security Guard in the Moscow embassy and his deputy were never disciplined for allowing their detachment to fall apart.

The Marine Corps has other less dramatic but more enduring problems around which debate revolves energetically and often quite fruitfully, notably in the pages of the *Marine Corps Gazette,* the intellectual forum of the corps. These break down into three categories: battlefield issues, administrative and bureaucratic concerns, and what might be loosely called "human" issues.

First, the battlefield. The marines have never been so well equipped and armed, from the grunt on the ground to the pilot in the air. Yet there are questions about how all this would shake down in a real war; there are questions of balance, of mobility, and of sustainability.

"Future battles will be very technological, very lethal, and very confused," says John Greenwood, a retired colonel in the Marine Corps and editor of the *Marine Corps Gazette*. "Survivability will be the major concern. There will be a greater need for cover, concealment, and dispersability. There will also be greater psychological problems and stress given the sheer weight of firepower. Guys will be overcome by fear."

Greenwood also suggests that anti-aircraft defenses will be so good that marine aviation, superb though it is, will not be able to provide as much support to the ground forces as it has in the past. There will be a need, he thinks, for more artillery, rockets, and unmanned aircraft. Communication and control systems, vital to the proper functioning of a marine air-ground task force, will be particularly vulnerable to enemy action, with a strong likelihood that they will break down, be jammed, or be taken out. The advance in military technology, Greenwood points out, is not confined to the first and second worlds. A number of Third World countries have sophisticated night vision systems, hand-held anti-aircraft missiles, and other modern weapons. Some even have a nuclear capability.

The Marine Corps, like any military unit in peacetime, is experiencing administrative and bureaucratic problems. The dog still wags the tail, but the tail is sometimes heavier and more wayward than it used to be. There are complaints within and outside the corps of excessive headquarter staffs, too many study groups, a surfeit of pen pushers, and a dearth of trigger pullers. There is much talk of "careerism," officers and staff NCOs who are keener on punching what they consider are the right tickets for promotion and the most comfortable niches for themselves and their families than on what might be best for the corps. Many NCOs complain of micromanagement by officers, and officers criticize a system of promotion that gives excessive power to their immediate superior, cramping initiative.

The third area of debate concerns the human material that is the lifeblood of the Marine Corps. As with everything else, the verdict cannot be given until the marines are tested once again in a major conflict. But some critics think the modern marine is a softer product than his forebears. A number of marine planners worry about the ability of the noninfantry marine to acquit himself on the battlefield, not because he cannot do his own specialist job or because he isn't motivated, but because he hasn't kept up his basic infantry skills. The race problem is no longer a major issue, but minorities are markedly under represented in the officer corps. The one black general, a Korea- and Vietnam-era aviator, has retired, and there is not another in sight. The Marine Corps has not yet come to terms with the role of women in its ranks though they constitute about 5 percent of the total force and are, by and large, even more gung ho than many of the males.

If anyone can solve problems and influence the direction of the corps, it is the commandant. The job is uniquely powerful and visible among the U.S. armed services. The commandant is chosen by a rather arcane selection process that involves the Secretary of the Navy, the Secretary of Defense, the outgoing commandant, and the President. His tenure is a presidential four-year term, and the man who holds it wields enormous power and inspires almost mythic veneration. He is at once the leader of a warrior caste, the head of a multibillion-dollar organization, and a member of the supreme military council in the land (the Joint Chiefs of Staff). There are, of course, institutional and other limits to what a commandant can do, and an entity as old as the United States Marine Corps tends to march to the sound of its own drum. But if the commandant decides to do something, it usually gets done, if not directly then by osmosis. A colonel who has watched commandants come and go put it this way: "The corps moves to the personality of the commandant."

The Marine Corps, despite its modern weaponry and its highly educated and much more worldly officer corps, retains a curiously old-fashioned flavor. The obsessions with short hair, big muscles, robotic rhetoric, and a zero-defect public image seem strange and unnecessary in a more relaxed era when no one seriously challenges its role, its professionalism, or its place in American society. Part of the old image, however, has changed: The corps is not the hard-drinking, foul-mouthed outfit of a bygone era. "Alcohol," according to one officer, "has been deromanticized in the Marine Corps." This does not mean that marines don't get drunk and trash the club occasionally, but there is a quieter, more serious atmosphere around this venerable institution, an atmosphere tinged at times with an almost religious intensity and devotion.

If there is an "ism" in the woodwork, it is "workaholism," which is good news for those the corps is designed to protect, if less fun for those doing the protecting. Sometimes the desire to make everything sound both perfect and enjoyable is carried too far. Marine language carries its own coding. When a young harassed officer is asked by a senior how his day went and replies, "Challenging!" one suspects he really means "Bloody awful!" By the same token other common superlatives such as "dynamite" probably mean "outstanding," and "outstanding" equals "good."

The zealousness of the Marine Corps, while helping to weld an effective and reliable fighting force, also produces zealots. The phenomenon of Ollie North seemed to divide the corps, with the younger officers and enlisted men rooting for him. Senior officers, disturbed by the sight of North in full uniform taking the Fifth Amendment and by the stories of marines getting in over their heads in a murky world far from the battlefield, appeared less enthusiastic. A former marine infantry officer who fought in World War II, commented: "North is a recognizable type in the Marine Corps. You can spot them—Naval Academy types, good minds, well-trained, but they love to save the world and think they know how to do it." Another former marine, a lieutenant general, commented dryly that the problem was that North "lacked adult supervision." supervision."

One of the most striking things about the marines is their *tightness.* There may be two hundred thousand of them on active duty around the globe and hundreds of thousands who served at some time or another, but they never forget the corps, and they remain loyal to each other. Marines bring back their dead, even if other marines are put in jeopardy and may die in the act of retrieval. Stanley Kubrick got that right in his movie *Full Metal Jacket* when the marines were prepared to sacrifice men in order to retrieve comrades killed by a sniper. British Royal Marines, no less tough and loyal, have a different view: a dead marine is a dead marine, and it is not worth sacrificing a live one to bring a dead one back. There is, as Victor Krulak points out in his book *First to Fight,* a primitive tribal feel about the Marine Corps: "Each generation [of marines] has its medicine men—keepers of the tribal mythology, protectors of the tribal customs, and guardians of the tribal standards."

In a conversation with a young black captain at the Marine Barracks in Washington, this idea was put another way. He had grown up in an army family on Okinawa. "As a kid I tried to hustle marines at pool tables," he said. "To me, they were the biggest, baddest, most tenacious and hardheaded young men that I had ever seen, and I wanted to be part of that. The marines called the corps the 'crotch,' and they bitched about it all the time. But if anyone outside the corps criticized it they'd be all over them like stink on shit. They loved the corps even when they wanted out."

This tightness translates into peer pressure as well as peer love. "The Marines have a way of making you afraid, not of dying, but of not doing your job," wrote Captain Bonnie Little in a last letter home before being killed on Tarawa in World War II.

A view from the outside and inside came from a British Royal Navy Harrier pilot, serving on an exchange program with a marine Harrier unit in Arizona. "There is too much 'positive criticism' in the U.S. Marine Corps," he said. "Everything tends to be 'outstanding,' 'super,' 'dynamic,' and so on. Back home, after an exercise, you get your tits hammered if things went wrong. You don't slash your wrists, but it's good for training. Also I find their organization cumbersome, with too much administration and headquarters staff. But in a war they'll do well because they're stubborn, and they believe in their history. They'll also outnumber and outgun their enemy, for sure, as they have always done. There's a cultural thing going for them, too—the American belief in democracy and the right to bear arms to defend it."

Marines know in their heart of hearts, despite their insecurity and paranoia about survival, that it is the *idea* of the corps that matters most. All long-living elite military units know this. The day-to-day concerns, the changing panorama of personalities, the exciting successes and embarrassing reverses, the passionate debates all consume energy. But as long as marines understand and nurture the idea of their corps it will survive and flourish.

While there are plenty of geopolitical and hardheaded defense imperatives that keep the United States Marine Corps in business, there is also something much less tangible but equally important. This is a sense of history. It is eloquently evoked in *The Story of the U.S. Marines*, a book written by George Hunt. Here he describes marine infantry on the move in Korea:

Day after day, the marines of the 7th Regiment trudged up the valley into the snows and winds. In their coats with pointed hoods they looked like helmeted men-of-arms in olden times. And with them trudged other columns of men who marched unseen and unheard. They marched to rolling drums and screeching fifes. Led by officers in powdered wigs, they marched in black boots and gaiters and hats with jaunty cockades. They marched in green coats with white cross belts, in deep blue ones with gold-trimmed belts, in dark green, mud-spattered brown, or in sweaty sun-bleached khaki. They were the marines of ten wars and more than two hundred battles already fought and won but never forgotten—of raids on enemy coasts; engagements at sea on the decks of proud frigates; countless skirmishes, storming parties, and landings in far-off places. They were the men who had made and handed down all the traditions that lay behind that trudging column in the valley, traditions of things endured and things accomplished.

Uniforms of the Marine Corps

Clockwise from top left
Officer, camouflage utilities with field jacket, web gear, and .45 pistol
Officer, evening dress B with boatcloak
Officer, service C with aiguillette and garrison cap
Officer, mess dress with aiguillette
SNCO, camouflage utilities
Officer, evening dress A
Drum major, United States Marine Band, full dress with mace
SNCO drill instructor, service C with sword
SNCO, blue-white dress A with sword
SNCO drill instructor service A with sword
Color guard with USMC battle colors
Assistant Director, United States Marine Band, full dress
Center photograph
Blue-white dress with M-1 rifle and fixed bayonet at ceremonial parade rest

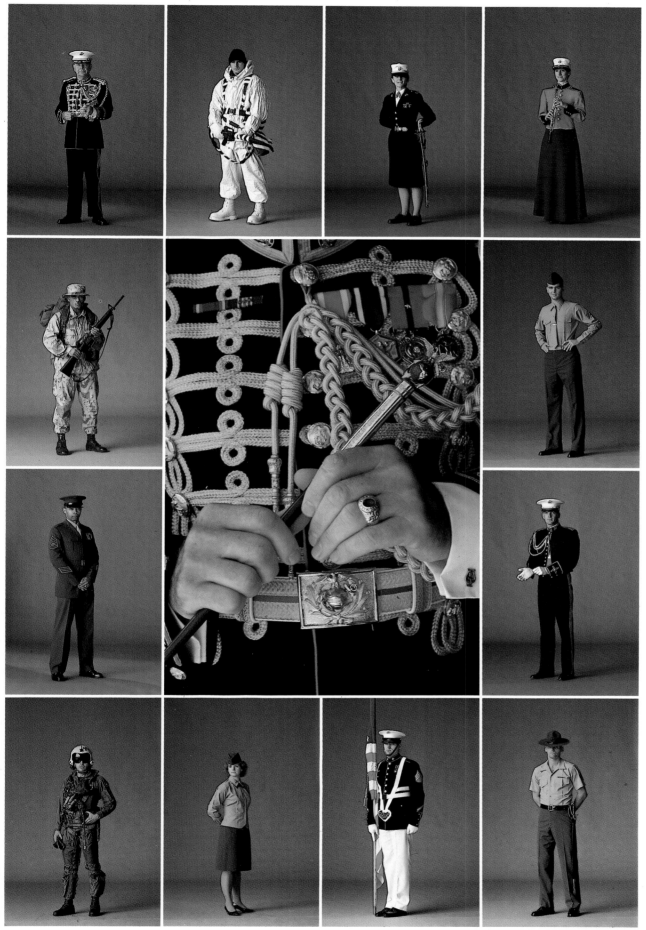

Clockwise from top left
Director, United States Marine Band, full dress
Lance corporal, arctic combat gear with watchcap and M-16 rifle
Officer, blue dress A with sword
Musician, United States Marine Band, special full dress with oboe
NCO, winter service B with garrison cap
Officer, evening dress B with aiguillette
SNCO drill instructor, service C with sword
Color guard blue-white dress A
Officer, service B
Aviator fixed wing flight suit with helmet
SNCO, service A with barracks cover
NCO, desert camouflage utilities with M-16 rifle
Center photograph
Director, United States Marine Band, full dress with Souza's baton

Clockwise from top left
Lance corporal, blue-white dress B with M-1 rifle
NCO, camouflage utilities with full field gear and M-16 rifle
Musician, United States Marine Band, full dress with field snare drum
NCO, blue dress B
Lance corporal, winter camouflage utilities with field jacket web gear and M-60 machine gun
Assistant Director, United States Marine Drum and Bugle Corps, red-white full dress
Winter service B with sweater
Officer, blue-white dress with sword
NCO, blue dress B
Officer, white dress B
Officer, blue dress B
Officer, service B with leather flying jacket
Center photograph
Detail of leather flying jacket

250

Clockwise from top left
Recon parachutist
Musician, United States
Marine Drum and Bugle
Corps, red-white dress
SNCO, service C with
slacks
Chesty VIII, USMC
mascot, with handler,
blue-white dress
Officer, service C with
barracks cover
SNCO, blue dress B, with
top coat and white gear
Lance corporal, blue
dress C
SNCO, evening dress
NCO, service B with
garrison cap
Officer, blue dress A
with topcoat and sword
USMC rifle team member
Officer, blue-white
dress A
Center photograph
Detail of USMC brass
buttons

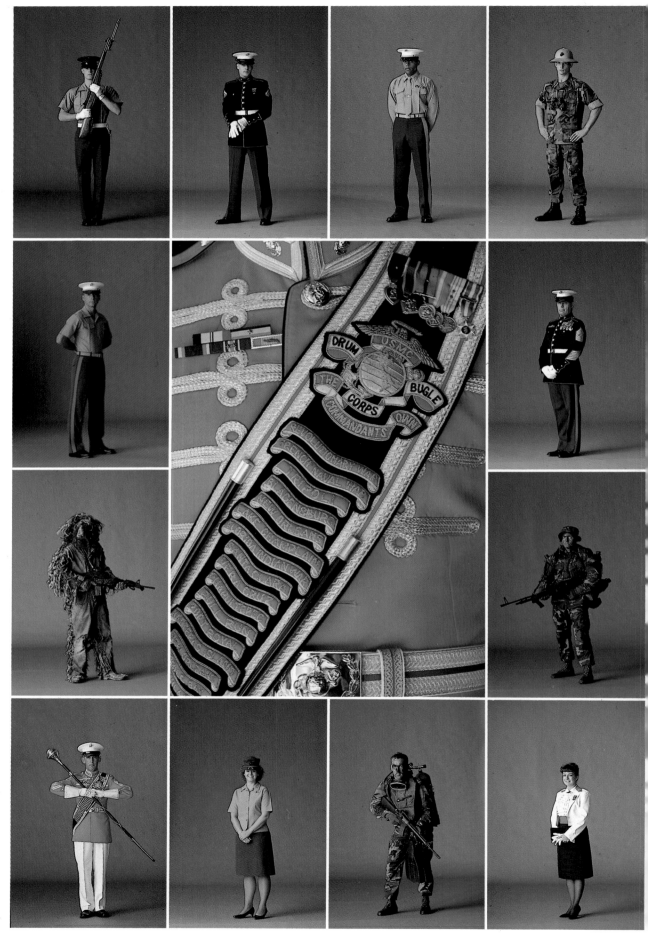

Clockwise from top left
NCO, service C with white gear, M-1 rifle and barracks cover
Lance corporal, blue dress B
Officer, winter blue dress C
NCO, camouflage utilities with pith helmet
SNCO, blue dress A
Recon camouflage with M-60 machine gun
Officer, mess dress
Recon scuba
Officer, summer service C
Drum major, United States Marine Drum and Bugle Corps, red-white full dress with mace
SNCO, scout sniper-observer, ghillie suit and M-16 rifle
Officer, summer blue dress C
Center photograph
Drum major, United States Marine Drum and Bugle Corps, baldric detail

252

Clockwise from top left
SNCO summer blue
dress D
Officer service A
NCO, United States
Marine Drum and Bugle
Corps, red-blues
SNCO, scout sniper,
ghillie suit with sniper
M-40A1 rifle
Officer, service A with
gloves and sword
Officer, white dress B
SNCO, service dress A
with garrison cap
Officer, blue dress A
with Sam Browne belt
and sword
Officer, camouflage
utilities with pistol belt
Officer, mess dress
SNCO, recon parachutist
Officer, blue-white dress
with sword
Center photograph
Officer's sword detail

HISTORICAL CHRONOLOGY

1775 The Second Continental Congress, sitting in Philadelphia on November 10, authorizes two battalions of "American Marines" to be formed to fight the British. The idea for creating a marine unit was hatched, tradition has it, in the Tun Tavern in Philadelphia. Samuel Nicholas, thirty-one years old, is given a captain's commission and put in command.

1776 On March 3 the marines make their first beach assault against British-held Bahamas. Rowing ashore in whaleboats, they encounter no opposition.

1778–79 Marines fight with John Paul Jones in the Atlantic and around the British Isles.

1783 The Revolutionary War ends, and there is peace with Britain. The "Continental Marines," as they become known, are disbanded.

1798 The modern Marine Corps is created by act of Congress on July 11, with headquarters in Philadelphia.

1800 William Ward Burrows is appointed "lieutenant colonel commandant" and founds the United States Marine Band, The President's Own.

1801 Burrows and President Jefferson choose the site for a new headquarters for the corps at 8th and I streets in southeast Washington, D.C.

1804 Burrows dies and is succeeded by Lieutenant Colonel Franklin Wharton.

1805 Lieutenant Presley Neville O'Bannon leads a small detachment of marines and other forces across the Libyan desert against the Pasha of Tripoli and ousts him. The pasha is replaced by his brother, who presents O'Bannon with a Mameluke sword that becomes the model for the ones that marine officers still carry.

1812–15 Britain and the U.S. go to war. Marines fight in the Atlantic, the Great Lakes, at Bladensburg in defense of Washington, and at New Orleans.

1818 Major Anthony Gale, a contentious figure with a drinking problem, takes over the corps after the death of Lieutenant Colonel Franklin Wharton, who had left Washington prematurely during the attack by the British.

1820 Gale is court-martialed and cashiered after quarreling with the Secretary of the Navy. (He is the only commandant who does not have his portrait hanging in the commandant's house at the Marine Barracks in Washington.) He is succeeded by Archibald Henderson, who will become the longest-serving commandant, remaining in the post until his death thirty-eight years later.

1824 A marine detachment from the Boston Navy Yard quells a riot in Boston's state prison.

1832 Sumatran pirates attack an American merchant ship in the East Indies, and marines take punitive action.

1834 On June 30, Congress passes an act defining more clearly the status, strength, and pay and rank structure of the Marine Corps.

1836 Marines, led by Commandant Henderson, fight against Seminole and Creek Indians in Florida and Alabama.

1844 A marine detachment lands near Canton, China, to protect the American community.

1846 The Mexican War begins, and First Lieutenant Archibald Gillespie is sent to Monterey in Mexican-held California by President Polk. Marines fight in several engagements that lead to the conquest of California.

1847 An American invasion of Mexico, with landing at Vera Cruz in March, is the marines' first large amphibious operation in conjunction with the navy and the army. On September 13 the marines assault the hill Chapultepec and occupy the Halls of Montezuma in the heart of Mexico City. In the late 1840s, marine officers and NCOs begin wearing a scarlet stripe on their dress trousers that is said to commemorate the blood shed by marines at Chapultepec. "The Marine Corps Hymn" also has its origins in the Mexican War.

1853 A marine detachment accompanies Commodore Perry on his first visit to Japan.

1856 Marines move into action again in Canton.

1857 Marines, led by Commandant Henderson, seventy-four years old, help suppress election riots in Washington, D.C.

1859 Henderson dies on January 6 and is succeeded by Lieutenant Colonel John Harris, sixty-eight years old. Marines, under the overall command of Lieutenant Colonel Robert E. Lee of the army, are sent down to Harpers Ferry, where John Brown, the antislavery activist, had seized the armory. The marines, led by First Lieutenant Israel Greene, charge the building, wounding and capturing Brown and releasing his hostages.

1861–65 The Civil War begins. A third of the corps' officers resign, most of them joining the Confederate States Marine Corps. The United States Marines, under their aged and lackluster commandant, John Harris, play a small and generally undistinguished part in the conflict. Harris dies in May 1864 and is succeeded by Major Jacob Zeilin, an experienced and more dynamic officer who is chosen over four senior officers.

1866 Congress considers abolishing the Marine Corps but finally decides to retain it.

1876 Brigadier General Zeilin retires as commandant and is replaced by Colonel Charles McCawley. During the 1870's marines are repeatedly used to quell labor and other civil disturbances in the eastern United States.

1880 John Philip Sousa is appointed director of the U.S. Marine Band and leads it for twelve years. He writes many marches, including "Semper Fidelis," which is to become the official Marine Corps march.

1891 Commandant McCawley retires, and Colonel Charles Heywood takes over.

1898 In the Spanish-American War a marine detachment is on the U.S.S. *Maine* when it blows up in Havana harbor. A marine battalion is sent to fight Spaniards in Cuba, landing at Guantanamo Bay. Sergeant John Quick wins a Medal of Honor at Cuzco.

1899 Marines move into action against rebels in the Philippines around Cavite and Subic Bay.

1900 During the Boxer Rebellion in China there is heavy fighting by marines in Tientsin and Peking in defense of the foreign communities and legations. Daniel "Fighting Dan" Daly wins the first of his two Medals of Honor.

1901 There is more fighting in the Philippines. The agonizing march to Samur takes place and is led by Major Waller.

1903 George Elliott becomes the new commandant.

1910 William Biddle takes over as commandant following Elliott's retirement.

1912 First Lieutenant Alfred Cunningham becomes the first marine pilot, flying a Curtiss seaplane.

1914 George Barrett becomes commandant, the first Naval Academy graduate to hold the post. Marines capture Vera Cruz, Mexico. World War I begins in Europe.

1915 Marines are sent to Haiti to fight rebels. Major Smedley Butler ("Old Gimlet Eye"), who had won a Medal of Honor at Vera Cruz, is awarded another one. Dan Daly also wins his second Medal of Honor in Haiti.

1916 A marine expeditionary force is sent to Santo Domingo to fight antigovernment rebels and bandits and remains there until 1924.

1917–18 The U.S. declares war on Germany on April 6, 1917. A marine brigade is sent to France in early 1918 to join the U.S. Army's Second Division. Marines fight with distinction in battles at Belleau Wood, Soissons, Saint Mihiel, Meuse-Argonne, and Blanc Mont. Brigadier General John Lejeune takes over the Second Division in July 1918, the first marine general to command an army division. Marine aviation, in its infancy, moves into action with a number of bombing missions in latter part of the war.

1920 Lejeune, another Naval Academy graduate, becomes commandant and remains in the position throughout the twenties. An innovative thinker, Lejeune is sometimes called the "father of the modern Marine Corps."

1921 Marines are detailed to guard the U.S. mails—trains and postal vans—following a spate of robberies.

1926 Marines are sent to Nicaragua for the second time to help the government. Their principal adversary is Augusto Cesar Sandino, a wily guerrilla leader; one of his most tenacious pursuers is First Lieutenant Lewis "Chesty" Puller, who wins the first of his five Navy Crosses there. The marines will not leave Nicaragua until 1933. The campaign sees the first use of close air support for ground troops by marine aviation.

1927 Marines are dispatched to China to reinforce foreign legations threatened by the civil war and remain there until 1938. These are the China Marines, who include a mounted troop known as the Horse Marines.

1929 Major General Lejeune retires and is succeeded by Wendell Neville, who dies in office a year later.

1930 Ben Fuller takes over the corps, much to the disappointment of Smedley Butler, who was the senior general in the Marine Corps at the time.

1934 John Russell becomes commandant, the last of five consecutive Naval Academy graduates to hold the position.

1936 Thomas Holcomb succeeds Russell as commandant.

1939 World War II begins in Europe.

1941 Japan attacks Pearl Harbor on December 7. Marine force surrenders on Wake Island after stiff resistance.

1942 The siege and fall of Corregidor and the Bataan "death march" in the Philippines take place. There are successful assaults on the Pacific islands of Tulagi (Edson's Raiders), Guadalcanal, and Makin (Carlson's Raiders).

1943 The battles of Bougainville, Tarawa, and New Britain take place.

1944 Alexander Vandegrift becomes commandant. There are the Pacific battles of Roi-Namur, Eniwetok, Saipan, Guam, Tinian, and Peleliu.

1945 The battles of Iwo Jima and Okinawa occur. Atom bombs are dropped on Hiroshima and Nagasaki, and Japan surrenders.

1945–47 Marines go to China again during the postwar occupation.

1947–50 Clifton Cates succeeds Vandegrift as commandant. Cuts are made in the Marine Corps budget and strength, and there are intraservice battles over the role of the corps.

1950–53 The Korean War begins, with marines prominent in battles in the Pusan perimeter, the Inchon landing, the Chosin Reservoir, and the "Punchbowl."

1952 Lemuel Shepherd takes over as commandant from Cates. Congress passes the Douglas-Mansfield Act, mandating that the peacetime Marine Corps should have no fewer than three active divisions and three aircraft wings.

1955 Randolph Pate is appointed commandant. A traditionalist, he reintroduces the swagger stick for officers and staff NCOs.

1956 At Ribbon Creek on Parris Island six recruits are drowned in the swamps during a night march. Marines land in Egypt to help evacuate foreign civilians during the Arab-Israeli War.

1958 Marines land in Lebanon during a political crisis.

1960 David Shoup takes over as commandant, selected by President Eisenhower over the heads of nine senior generals.

1964 Wallace Greene, a Naval Academy graduate, succeeds Shoup.

1965 Marine forces are sent to Dominican Republic following civil strife. Marines are also sent to Da Nang in South Vietnam, the first American ground-combat forces to enter the country.

1967 Leonard Chapman succeeds Greene as commandant. The first battle of Khe Sanh takes place in Vietnam.

1968 The Tet Offensive, the second battle of Khe Sanh, and the battle of Hue City mark this year.

1969 Marine forces in Vietnam are reduced.

1972 Robert Cushman becomes commandant in January. North Vietnam launches its Easter Offensive.

1973 The Paris peace accords are signed, ending American involvement in Vietnam.

1975 Louis Wilson is appointed commandant. Saigon falls to North Vietnam. Cambodian forces attack the *Mayaguez*, an American container ship. Marines participate in a confused reprisal raid to rescue the crew. The Marine Corps celebrates its two hundredth birthday.

1976 A recruit dies at San Diego, leading to reform in recruit training.

1979 Robert Barrow becomes commandant. Marines take part in an abortive Iran raid to free U.S. embassy hostages.

1983 P.X. Kelley is appointed commandant. Marines are sent to Lebanon as part of an international peacekeeping force. Barracks in Beirut are blown up by a suicidal truck bomber, killing 241 marines.

1984 Marines take part in an invasion of Grenada.

1987 A marine guard in the U.S. embassy in Moscow is convicted of spying for the Soviet Union. Alfred Gray becomes commandant.